GW01451305

What motivated me to write this book was a deep desire to share the facts, which have been gathered from various sources and the result of my own experiment on the power of mind as a research fellow of Rajyoga Education and Research Foundation. In this book, I have tried to explain the great fundamental truths of human mind. Although psychologists and mind experts have explained it partially in their own languages, but I have tried to explain it in common man's language which can be easily understood by anyone.

BEST BOOKS ON PERSONALITY DEVLOPMENT

MANAGEMENT GURU BHAGWAN SHRI RAM
Dr. Sunil Jogi

Management Guru Bhagwan Shri Ram is a marvellous book written by the acclaimed author Dr. Sunil Jogi. In this book, a number of management tips of Bhagwan Ram have been discussed in details. Management Guru Ram achieved unique management skills through self-restraint and politeness. He is a theist. So, this book will certainly be a source of inspiration to the new generation.   **Price : 95.00**

Book By: Joginder Singh (Former CBI Director)
SUCCESS MANTRA

This book is a masterpiece by Sh. Joginder Singh, IPS (Retd) who is a former Director of the CBI. Hailing from a poor farmer's family, he scaled the pinnacles of success through sheer motivation and hard work. The saga of success he has enunciated through his win-win story is worth emulating for any young aspirant for achievements and glory in life: to be on top!
Price : 150.00

HOW TO EXCEL WHEN CHIPS ARE DOWN
Excellent suggestions with suitable examples have been cited in the book which will guide youngesters about the importance of objective thinking and to erase unwanted thoughts from their memory.   **Price : 95.00**

FOR A BETTER TOMORROW
This magnum opus by Sh. Joginder Singh is a treatise on self improvement. This win-win sory is based on the secrets of success as to how to become an achiever. And the success mantra that he espouses for you. Make the best of all opportunities; dream big and work hard-dreams will turn sheer realities.   **Price : 150.00**

WINNING WAYS
The mantra he unveils for success, through this book, is potent enough to lift the young and ambitious to the highest peaks. These winning tips will inspire your morale to achieve greater glories - you simply need to tune up your mindset and hone your skills.
•••••••••••••• **Price : 150.00**

Books By: Dr. Ujjwal Patni
GREAT WORDS, WIN HEARTS

Great Words, Win Hearts will tell you the powerful ways to get noticed, to get heard, to impress the listeners, to remove public and stage fear. The author, Dr. Ujjwal Patni assures that after reading this book every common man can speak effectively and strongly, everywhere and everywhere without any fear, hesitation or inferiority complex.   **Price : 150.00**

WINNERS & LOSERS
This book can shake you, hurt you, make you feel ashamed, arouse you, encourage you or bring forward bitter facts.   •••••••••••••• **Price : 150.00**

INVISIBLE DOCTOR
B.K. Chandrashekhar

It is a unique book written by B.K. Chandrashekhar to shed light on the nature of human mind and its role in health. It explores the missing dimension of medicine. The concept of Invisible Doctor is a tool in the hand of physicians treating their patients. This will definitely magnify the healing process alongwith medicine. In this book, the Invisible Doctor has given various tips to cure various diseases such as T.B., breast cancer, amoebiasis, depression, dyspepsia etc. through Neurobics.
Price : 110.00

DIAMOND BOOKS X-30, Okhla Industrial Area, Phase-II, New Delhi-110020,
Phones : 41611861- 65, 40712100, Fax: 011- 41611866
E-mail : Sales@dpb.in, Website: www.dpb.in

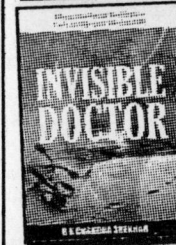

Science of Mind Simplified

(A to Z Steps of Stress Management and Healthy Living)

B.K. Chandra Shekhar

FUSION BOOKS

ISBN : 81-8419-076-X

© **Author**

Publisher   : **Diamond Pocket Books (P) Ltd.**
                       X-30, Okhla Industrial Area, Phase-II
                       New Delhi-110020
Phone   : 011-41611861, 40712100
Fax   : 011-41611866
E-mail   . : sales@dpb.in
Website   : www.dpb.in
Revised Edition : 2010
Printer   : Adarsh Printers,
                       Navin Shahdara, Delhi-32

Science of Mind Simplified
By : B.K. Chandra Shekhar

DEDICATION

Dedicated with reverence to
"Almighty GOD",
The Supreme father of
all souls and the Source of
True Knowledge.

PREFACE

To a question, "Who is flying kite?"
A boy replies, "I am flying the kite."
The tail of the kite says, "I am flying the kite."
The wind says, "I am flying the kite."
The string says, "I am flying the kite."
Voice of the Lord said, "Oh children, we are flying the kite."
Hence, the prayer says, "let us all be enlightened."
We can relax in this unjust world only when we teach ourselves and others to strengthen our strength and weaken our weaknesses.

Human beings possess one special faculty that none of the other living beings have. That is the ability to think. A computer on the ground controls the satellite situated thousands of kilometers away. It can carry out all the instructions set by human beings perfectly like a slave. But it cannot think. **The only living beings on earth that are capable of thinking are human beings.** But how many of us utilise this thinking capacity? **We have guided weapons and satellites but unguided mind.** We have become slave of our own mind. The knowledge in this book will definitely trigger your power of mind to work as guided by self.

Whatever is our weakness, if we do not identify with it, the toxic centre in us will lose its grip on us. We have infinite riches within our reach. To gain them, all we have to understand is our nature of mind and behold the treasure house of infinity within us. There is a storehouse within us from which we can extract everything we need to live life gloriously, joyously and peacefully.

A magnetised piece of iron will lift about twelve times of its own weight but if demagnetised the same piece of iron will not lift even a feather. In the same way, the people who have magnetic mind power, live their lives with full faith and confidence but those who have not understood their mind, grope in the dark and remain full of fears and doubts.

What motivated me to write this book was a deep desire to share the facts, which have been gathered from various sources and the result of my own experiment on the power of mind as a research fellow of Rajyoga Education and Research Foundation. I have tried to explain the great fundamental truths of human mind. Although psychologists and mind experts have explained it partially in their own languages, but I have tried to explain it in common man's languages which can be easily understood by anyone.

Before I close, I wish to share with the readers of the book about the healing powers of the mind because a personal healing will always be the most convincing evidence of the power of mind. Like most of us, I faced many depressing situations. Physically I had suffered from cancer, hepatitis-C, fibrosis of lever and diabetes. I met with serious accidents also. Many times I stood in utter darkness. I coped with darkness through the power of mind and got unbelievably great results. The diseases were gone and I became normal again. I also improved my memory power by improving concentration and the power of my mind. In this book, I share the cruxes of my experiments and conclusions of my experiences in stress management. Read this book carefully, earnestly and lovingly. It can help you in amazing ways in managing your stress and maintaining peak level performances. It may be the turning point of your life. Let wonders happen in our lives. Keep on until the day breaks and the darkness flee away.

– *B.K. Chandra Shekhar*
E-mail: bkcshekhar@yahoo.in

CONTENTS

1

SCIENCE OF MIND

One speciality of all sciences – biological, geological, astronomical, natural, physical, medical etc.– is that they have their own methodology. A common feature of the methodology of all sciences is **observation**. Observation is generally the first step in all-scientific exploration. Observation stirs the mind and a chain of thoughts and ideas emerges from our memory bank, which is also known as subconscious/unconscious mind. Observation also gives a fillip to a person's rational thoughts, intuitions, imaginations and ability of focusing or concentrating on a subject of search.

Thus, observation leads to assumption, postulation, experimentation, interpretation, theory making or formulae making or quantification and calibration, so that anyone can understand the finding in the rational manner, can repeat the experiment, verify the truth and reproduce the result. Therefore, science is the result of person's abilities, which are only the manifestations of **consciousness at various levels**. So consciousness is the first or the prime reality and without it all other realities (physical, chemical, mechanical etc.) would remain unknown.

Why is there a need to study the Science of Mind?

People spend years in the study of science and the cosmos but they hardly spend any worthwhile and fruitful time to understand the self or consciousness, mind, intellect and human memory system. They do not spare some moments from their other pursuits to know the answer to the most important question: 'Who Am I?' They spend their whole energy in knowing what is material, but spare no time to know this non physical and non material reality which is called 'Meta Science' or the scientific knowledge of self without which one would have only a distorted, incomplete or fractured and fragmented world view. We all wish to experience peace, happiness, bliss and try to avoid that which is painful, unpleasant, frustrating or negative. Also, the self or the consciousness has emotions, such as love, mercy etc. whereas the material, such as the table, does not have any emotion. The quality of one's life is intimately connected to one's emotions. So, the study of Meta Science or science of mind or spiritual science that can enable us to know the science of happy living is utmost necessary.

Knowledge of the Science of Mind is a Must to Avoid Trauma

If we wish to avoid pit falls and personal traumas in life, the study of consciousness, the self or the spiritual laws, related to it, is necessary. We can neglect these and have mental tensions. **We can win a Nobel prize in life but the notable prize in life is constant peace and bliss.** Without this life is nothing but a slow suicide. One may know all sciences more than all classical scientists had or modern scientists have, but one may be a failure in life, if one does not have the light of knowledge, which leads to self-fulfilment and to ultimate goal, life becomes dark and hopeless.

Science without a Conscience may be Destructive

One may employ scientific principles to devise weapons of mass killing or may employ such ways of manufacturing as may pollute the environment, disturb ecology and make the world a veritable hell. Thus, one has to pay heed to moral aspect of one's action, which are creative and can make the world a better place to live in.

We must, therefore, have a **robust conscience** if we wish to avoid that which is liable to lead us to bad. Besides the five senses, we must use the sixth sense namely, the moral sense or conscience. We may or may not be able to win a **Nobel Prize** but we must have a **Noble Prize,** i.e. values which make life valuable and noble. And it is science of mind or knowledge of self that enables us to know and do this.

All these kinds of sciences play a complementary role. We should never forget that sciences give man enormous power. **If the head and the hands, which use that power, have no calm judgement and self-control, the power can cause great havoc.** The required self control, discipline, calm judgement and stability of mind comes from spiritual wisdom, moral science and practice of meditation.

So, in order to make a happy blend of the two, science and spirituality must work in unison to end social accidents, personality clashes, mental tensions and depressions.

Various Facets of the Science of Mind

The Science of mind deals with the following subjects in detail–

1. Science of self,
2. Inner mechanism of Mind, Intellect and Memory,
3. Mind and Brain relationship,
4. Soul, Mind, Brain and Body relationship,
5. Inner Body and Physical Body relationship,
6. Subtle Energy Centres and Aura,
7. Moral science,
8. Spiritual Powers,
9. Law of Nature,
10. Cosmic rays and the role of Supreme,
11. A new and perfect world order,
12. Art of Happy and Healthy living,
13. Goal and Role of life,
14. Harmony with science and spirituality,
15. Solution of all problems,
16. Eternal Cycle of Soul and Nature,
17. Healing power of Mind,
18. Purification of Mind for Pure Nature,
19. Telepathy and Telekinesis,
20. Concentration and Will Power and so on.

●●●

2

SCIENCE OF SELF

(I) Science of Self (Being)

As the study of the system of human body is called **physical science**, in the same manner the study of being is called **metaphysical science**, which is also known as **spiritual science or the Science of Mind**. Just like an **ATOM** is made up of **protons, electrons and neutrons**, similarly **ATMA** consists of three faculties called **Mind, Intellect, and Impressions in Memory (subconscious/unconscious mind)**.

The **Study of Atoms is Science and Study of Atma is called Spiritual Science.**

ATOM   ATMA

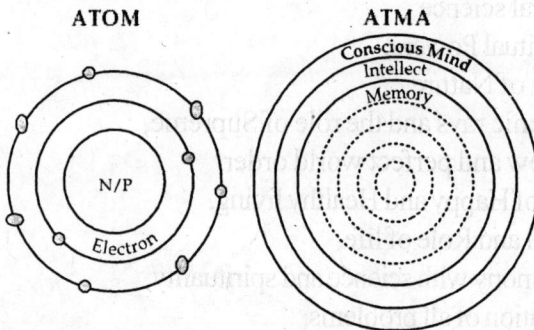

Human being – not one but two

When I say – I am Ram or Rahman, I mean the name of my body by which I am identified and called. If I say my father, my brother, wife or friend, it indicates their relationship with me. When I say my house, my car, my table, all these indicate my belongings. When I say I am a doctor, an engineer or a teacher, it indicates the acquired scientific and systematic knowledge for becoming a professional to earn my livelihood. When I say my head, my ears, my eyes, I mean these are the organs of my body. My relations, my body, my possessions are different from me though they belong to me. I make different uses of my body and its organs. Even the brain cannot think, decide, perceive and perform on its own. It is an inanimate component of the 'being', which performs these functions with the help of the brain and gross body. As all goods are meant for other's use, similarly the physical body is not created for its own use. It is for the use of the conscient entity known as 'being or soul'.

The soul is a sparkling point of conscient energy that empowers the entire body to monitor and perform all physical activities. The soul harmonizes the growth of body. When the soul (the master) leaves the body, the latter loses its awareness, ability to think, decide, act, react and experience. All including bodily functions ceases with the departure of 'being' from human.

So, soul is the life force in the living human body. It is situated in the centre of the forehead in level with hypothalamus and close to all the sense organs and acts through them. In layman's language, soul lives in the middle of the forehead. That is why, most people in India apply 'tilak' or 'bindi' on their forehead, as it is true symbol of the self being in the forehead.

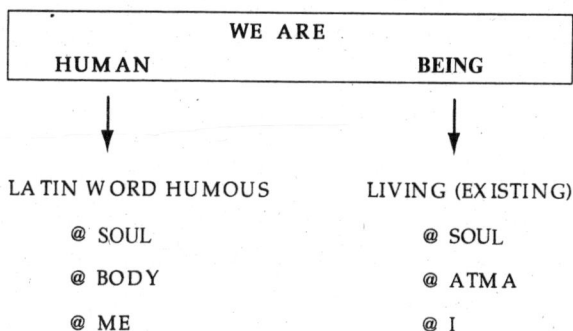

WE ARE	
HUMAN	BEING

↓	↓
LATIN WORD HUMOUS	LIVING (EXISTING)
@ SOUL	@ SOUL
@ BODY	@ ATMA
@ ME	@ I

Albert Einstein said, "Science without spirituality is blind and spirituality without science is lame." Both 'lame' and 'blind' want to have a taste of grapes but can not until both co-operate and co-ordinate with each other.

The basic study of science revolves around atoms. The word 'atom' has come from a Greek word called atomos, which means indivisible or a thing which can not be further sub divided. Atom is the smallest non-living physical entity.

From the very same word 'atomos' the word *'atma'* has also come which means the smallest living metaphysical entity.

Life of a human being is the perfect example of the blend of 'atoms' and *atma*.

ATOMOS (A GREEK WORD WHICH MEANS INDIVISIBLE)

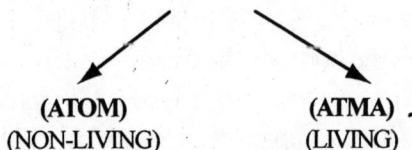

(ATOM)	(ATMA) .
(NON-LIVING)	(LIVING)

The word 'human' has come from a Latin word 'humous' which means soil which is further made up of millions of atoms and our body or me is made up of more than 60 trillions of these atoms. The word 'being', as per dictionary, means any thing which is existing, which is I or *atma* or soul.

(II) System of Human Being

There are two systems of human being. These are:

a. System of Human

b. System of Being (Inner System)

(a) *System of Human and Their Respective Functioning Organs*

There are eight systems in human body. Each system of human body has got its respective organs to function. For example, bones and muscles for skeleton system, billion of neurons and brain for nervous system, lungs for respiratory system, heart for circulatory system, stomach for digestive system, all glands for secretion of hormones and enzymes for endocrine system, sex organs for reproductive system and so on. It is well understood by the following table.

SYSTEM OF HUMAN BODY	RESPECTIVE ORGANS
1. Skeleton system	Bones and muscles
2. Nervous system	Brain & neurons
3. Respiratory system	Lungs
4. Circulatory system	Heart
5. Digestive system	Stomach
6. Endocrine system	All glands
7. Reproductive & immune system	Reproductive organs & WBC
8. Excretory system	Skin & excretory organs

(b) *System of "Being" and Respective Faculties*

The unique thing about the intrinsic abilities of 'being' is that, not a single other physical body or anything else is made of matter (like computer or calculator) that possesses these abilities except the soul. These are:

(1) The ability to think or wish or will or create emotions through conscious mind (in Hindi called – *Mann*). This is **thought system** of human being.

(2) The ability to analyse, understand or investigate, visualise or realise and to judge through the intellect (in Hindi called– *buddhi*). This is **control system** of being.

(3) The ability to retain impressions of past thoughts in the form of attitudes, moods, habits or resolves (in Hindi called – *Sanskars*) in its memory bank (known as subconscious mind and unconscious mind). This is **memory system** of being.

This is explained by the following table–

SYSTEM OF BEING	RESPECTIVE FACULTIES
Thought system	Conscious Mind
Control system	Intellect
Memory system	Sub-conscious Mind & Unconscious Mind

Thought System of Mind: Conscious mind is one of the faculties of the soul, which receives and creates thoughts and emotions. It receives thoughts and emotions either from sense organs of the body (eyes, ears, nose, tongue and skin) or from internal faculties like subconscious or unconscious mind.

(III) Mind Control System of the Intellect

The faculty by which the soul can select its desired thoughts and emotions is INTELLECT. The expression's "will power" is often used to refer our ability to put our ideas into practice. We know it is for our well-being and to resist activities, which are harmful. This is directly related to the soul's intellectual strength. When we speak of weakness or strength of the soul, we are referring to the intellect. In the case of a weak soul it is almost as if the intellect plays no part in determining which thoughts should arise in the mind, but they seem to come as if pushed by the impressions of subconscious mind or are triggered by the atmosphere around or the moods of others. On the contrary, a powerful soul enjoys the experience of its own choice regardless of the external stimuli. Thus, intellect performs three functions:

• Analyse, discern and discriminate
• Visualise several images related to the thoughts
• Judge or decide.

In other words, we can say that the intellect is gifted by soul with three powers:

Power to Discriminate, Power to Visualise and Power to Judge: Out of these three powers, power to visualise is the most important. That is why, intellect is also called 'the third eye' or 'eye' of knowledge and this is the eye of soul.

(IV) Memory System by Memory Bank

Now let us see the last faculty the subconscious mind and unconscious mind, which is called memory bank. Impressions of every action, observation and visualisation in subconscious mind are called Memory. In Sanskrit language, these dispositions or unconscious memories, which are the result of previous actions, are called *sanskars*. It is these, which give unity to the self. The self coordinates the information received from various senses into various parts of the brain and gives it an experimental unity without which the encoded memory would be meaningless.

Thus, when the conscious personality has its memories at subliminal or infra liminal level then it can be designated as subconscious or unconscious mind.

Subconscious mind has the power to do anything on the basis of information lying with it. It is the power of the subconscious mind that makes our heart beats 72 times per minute regularly for up to 100 years. It is well known to psychologists that we can consciously be aware of only 72 items at a time. But our subconscious mind can be aware of a large number of items at a time. For example; at any time, the subconscious mind is aware of many body functions including blood pressure, heartbeats, body temperature, chemical balances, blood flow, taking care of emergencies etc. **The subconscious mind is not under our conscious control.**

(V) Requirement of Human Body and Being

Requirement of 'Body' is quantitative: *Food, Cloth and Shelter.* Requirement of 'Being' (Soul) is qualitative as follows:

(a) *Primary Qualities*

We are originally a point of sentient light fully charged with spiritual (metaphysical) energy that naturally manifests as truth (knowledge), peace, love, joy, purity, power and bliss (balance) when we first come into this world. *These innate qualities or attributes of the soul are so basic that they themselves are the basis of all virtues and powers.*

Truth: An original attribute of the soul and the supreme soul is the true knowledge of the self, the Supreme and the 'eternal drama'. It is represented by the primary colour – indigo.

Peace: An original attribute of the soul and the supreme soul is peace, which is represented by the primary colour – Blue.

Love: Another original attribute of the soul and the supreme soul is love, which is represented by green colour – a mixture of blue and yellow.

Joy or Happiness: Yet another original attribute of the soul and the supreme soul is joy or happiness, which is represented by yellow, a primary colour.

Purity: The original attribute of the soul and the supreme soul is represented by orange colour – a mixture of yellow and red. Hence, in the state of purity there is a balance of power and joy.

Spiritual Power: Another original attribute of the soul and the supreme soul is power, which is represented by the primary colour – Red. The eight powers are different shades of red colour.

Bliss: The core attribute of the soul and the supreme soul is represented by violet colour – a mixture of red and indigo. Hence, in this state of being we are in a state of balance between truth and power. A blissful soul is full of both wisdom and spiritual powers.

(b) The Secondary Qualities of the Soul

Virtues are secondary qualities springing from myriad combinations of the seven basic attributes mentioned above. Another aspect of the secondary qualities, which come into play more frequently in our day-to-day life, is that these are linked to human relationships. These are as follows:

Discipline	Introvertness	Tirelessness	Detachment
Honesty	Self-confidence	Appreciation	Obedience
Generosity	Humility	Determination	Farsightedness
Orderliness	Sweetness	Fearlessness	Aloofness
Reality	Serenity	Egolessness	Purity
Good wish	Coolness	Sobriety	Mercifulness
Truthfulness	Contentment	Worrylessness	Asceticism
Politeness	Simplicity	Benevolence	Observer state
Equality	Tolerance	Co-operation	Royalty

(VI) Integrated, Action by All the Three Systems of Being

The five sense organs by which conscious mind receives information in the form of thoughts, emotions and desires are received by intellect where they are analysed, visualised and judged for the best possible actions. And then the body executes the actions through the motor organs. Now these actions are again observed by the sense organs and are registered as impressions in the memory system or the subconscious mind. This memory system supplies data and information to the conscious mind as and when registered. This process keeps taking place automatically day-in and day-out.

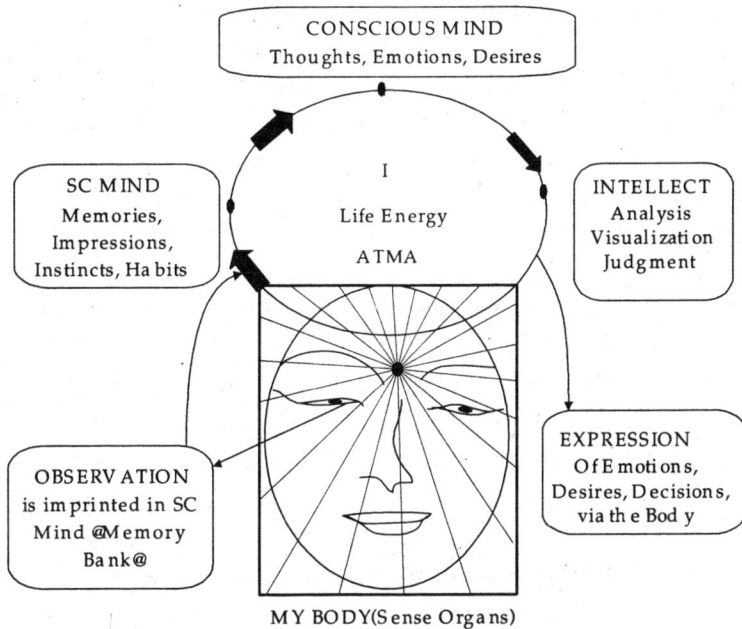

```
                    CONSCIOUS MIND
                 Thoughts, Emotions, Desires

   SC MIND              I                 INTELLECT
   Memories,        Life Energy            Analysis
   Impressions,        ATMA             Visualization
   Instincts, Habits                      Judgment

                                        EXPRESSION
   OBSERVATION                          Of Emotions,
   is imprinted in SC                Desires, Decisions,
   Mind @Memory                         via the Body
   Bank@

                 MY BODY(Sense Organs)
```

Let us take the example of a person learning to drive a car for the first time. The conscious mind through the sense organs gathers information on the techniques of driving.

These are analysed, visualised and judged by the control system and the driving action is controlled by the motor organs like hands, legs etc. These actions are observed by the sense organs and the impression of driving technique is registered in our memory or subconscious mind. From now onwards, the information to the conscious mind is fed both by subconscious mind and sense organs and to our surprise; after some time subconscious mind feeds 95 percent of the information and remaining 5 percent is fed by the sense organs.

Imagine a situation, during learning how to drive a car, when the instructor switches on the music system on the first day itself. The pupil finds it hard to concentrate and will find the music to be a disturbance. But after a few days when he becomes comfortable, without music he will get bored and ask for it. The reason is very simple. When the subconscious mind takes over, sense organs remains idle. This is the reason why a person goes to the bathroom automatically after waking up in the morning or the hand automatically goes to the alarm clock before he goes to sleep.

Out of all these, the most important function of the intellect is power of creative visualisation. It is the place where all the inventions takes place. Let me give some examples to drive home this point. Sir Isaac Newton saw an apple falling from a tree and visualised constantly and creatively why it falls down on the earth instead of going up in the sky. And this led to the theory of Gravitation.

It is well known that physicians use the power of visualisation to cure diseases by giving patients "placebo" with no real medicinal values, the patients are told otherwise, and the patients are cured with visualisation only.

A layman uses less than 1 percent of the power of intellect. An intellectual uses only 3 percent of his intellect. Scientists and researchers use only 10 percent of their intellect. While 90 percent of the intellect is still unused.

'IMPRESSIONS' are the genetic coding of the soul: Just as the metabolic activities of the cell body are based on the genetic information held in the nucleus, the quality of

mental activities of thoughts, desires, feelings, visions etc. are primarily based on impressions.

'INTELLECT' can change the genetic code of impressions: Just as the cell membrane selectively permit different molecules of nutrients into the cell body, similarly the intellect acts as a screening and monitoring device determining which influences from the environment should be processed and which one to be ignored. It also determines which thoughts, desires or vision prompted by impressions (*sanskars*) should be acted upon. The intellect can change the genetic code of impressions by focusing its attention on the original attributes and causing pure, virtuous thoughts to emerge on the mental screen. It can weaken negative (IMPRESSIONS) sanskaras by not allowing the related thoughts to reach at the level of action.

When the power of discrimination of the intellect is weak, the negative *sanskaras*, the negative vibrations of the environment and moods of other people find easy access on the mind making it very turbulent and peaceless.

VII Objective Mind and Subjective Mind
(A) Objective Mind
Conscious mind and intellect both are known as objective minds because they deals with outward objects. The objective mind is aware of the objective world. Its media of observation is our physical sense. Our intellect, one of the faculties of objective mind is our guide and director in our contact with our environment. We gain knowledge through our five senses. Our objective mind learns through observation, education and its association with past experiences of memory.

The greatest function of the objective mind is performed by intellect. It is of reasoning, visualising and decision making.
(B) Subjective Mind
Subconscious mind is also referred to as subjective mind. It is aware of its environment, but not by means of physical senses. It perceives by intuition. It is the seat of emotions and the storehouse of memory. It performs the highest functions when our objective

senses are not functioning. In other words, it is that intelligence that makes itself known when the objective mind is suspended or in a sleepy or drowsy state or in alpha or delta state.

Coordination Between Objective and Subjective Mind: When intellect, one of the faculties of objective mind withdraws from conscious mind, that is from sensory organ observations, and starts using its most important power of visualisation in coordination with subjective mind, there is a drastic reduction in brain waves from beta activities to alpha, theta and delta. In alpha, theta and delta waves, the third eye elevates itself with the capacity of clairvoyance and clairaudience. It can see and hear events that are taking place elsewhere. Sometimes, it leaves our body, travels to a distant lands and brings back information that is often of the most exact and truthful nature. The third eye with low brain waves can read the thoughts of others, read the contents of sealed envelopes or intuit the information on a computer disc without using disk drive. All these happen when intellect is deeply connected with subjective mind; that is subconscious mind, because the subconscious mind has all the impressions of past, present and future of our life. **Intellect with its full potential can even see in the subjective mind, what is going to happen.**

Once, we understand the interaction between the objective and subjective minds, we are in a better position to learn the true art of happiness and peaceful living. The habitual thinking of our objective mind establishes deep grooves in our subjective mind. If your habitual thoughts are harmonious, peaceful and constructive, your subjective mind will respond by creating harmony, peace and constructive conditions.

Our objective mind (intellect) or the third eye serves as the watchman at the gate who protects our subjective mind from false impressions. The reason is that our subjective mind is very sensitive to suggestion. It simply reacts to the impressions given to it by our third eye.

●●●

3

SCIENCE OF THOUGHTS AND EMOTIONS

Conscious mind is one of the faculties of the soul, which receives and creates thoughts, desires, images, ideas, feelings and emotions. It receives the thoughts and emotions either from sense organ of the body (eyes, ears, nose, tongue and skin) or from internal faculties called subconscious or unconscious mind also known as memory bank. So, the thoughts in conscious mind are the seeds of actions and experiences. When there is a thought of desire for pure experience, coupled with the realisation of the importance of quality of thought, then naturally those seeds will be selected which will bear the desired fruit. The desire may be for peace, knowledge, contentment, love, power, joy, insight or any one of the positive experiences may be savoured to feel those past happy moments from the subconscious mind. Of course, there will be an aim to control or eradicate those thoughts and impressions which are the seeds of disharmony and peacelessness.

Functions of the Conscious Mind

Thoughts, imaginations, creation of ideas, sensations, desire, feelings and emotions are essential functions of the emotional self. The soul uses the conscious mind as a screen or field on which thoughts, desires, sensations and ideas are projected as images. An experience, feeling or emotions, of these images is the impact of these projections, which is also known as a state of mind.

If I want to feel good, I have to have the type of thoughts that bring the quality of goodness. **However, conscious mind is subject to the whims and inconsistencies of the intellect.**

Wherever the intellect roams, the conscious mind automatically follows, producing all of its essential functions. The core beliefs described therein are based on the emotional needs of the '**inner child**' **(active impressions in memory of a soul)** and these determine how we will interact with others. Based on this need, we face people with openness and optimism or with fear, despair, hatred, hostility etc.

Because of the unfulfilled need for safety, love or self-identity we tend to believe that we are unworthy of anything that would provide these. Then our thoughts, actions and beliefs are in reaction to our core belief, either striving to counter its influences or succumbing to that belief. In the face of an emotional need, our heart rules our head. Logic can neither sway, nor argue the 'inner child' into submission because our children's emotional needs far outweigh intellectual reasoning. The foundation of the emotional self is love that comes from within, assuring us that we are now safe and taken care of. When we clear away the painful, non-living beliefs and behaviours, the 'inner child' and ourselves open up for nurturance by God by divinising the intellect and filling the mind with positive emotions.

Types of Thoughts and Emotions Received by the Conscious Mind

Subconscious mind or memory bank is the store of all impressions of our experiences and actions, though we are not aware of them. They are latent. Human personality is adjusted by these latencies or potentials only. These latencies or hidden potentials can be compared to an iceberg. Hardly ten percent of the iceberg is visible above the surface of the water. More than ninety percent of the iceberg is invisible beneath the water line. Therefore, even powerful storm cannot change the direction of an iceberg because of the strong undercurrents running in opposite direction of the powerful storm and controlling more than ninety percent of the iceberg. Similarly, what we know about other's character or behaviour is only a tiny amount of the ten percent visible. Ninety percent of our invisible personality, which is within the subconscious mind and unknown to even ourselves is controlled by some very strong undercurrents and is the driving force of our personality in a particular direction. This is called **ACTIVE UNDERCURRENTS OR ACTIVE IMPRESSION OR ACTIVE SUB CONSCIOUS MEMORY**, which is a record of small and big events of the recent past life or past events of this life since childhood or impressions of previous birth, which influence our personality and keep moulding our character subconsciously. Day to day impressions, which are recorded by our visualisation and associations, are also part of the active memory. Thus these active impressions (memory) work like an under current, which determine the direction of our present attitudes, belief, fears, prejudices and all subconscious behaviour. This is also called the inner child who is very arrogant and outweighs intellect appeals.

It is the subconscious memory which gives a man a unified character or personality from moment to moment in its normal state of wakefulness and these active impressions keep coming in our conscious mind in the forms of thought energy, desires, feelings and emotions which is called consciousness which further determines our state of mind, attitudes, visions and influences our decisions and actions which further strengthens the same impressions in our active memory which is called a strong belief and then beliefs will be automatically reflected from time to time through our characters and behaviours.

Following are the **six types of thoughts and emotions** that keep coming to our conscious mind from active or inactive memories of our subconscious or unconscious mind **at the rate of more than 30 thoughts per minute.**

(A) Waste Thoughts

These thoughts are not related to any necessary or productive work. Such thoughts may not release toxic chemicals yet waste time and energy. These thoughts are mainly connected with the past happenings and events upon which the conscious mind and intellect keeps on brooding. These thoughts even mix up with the thoughts coming from sense organs and create gloomy images about the unknown future or start day dreaming and making castles in the air. Frequent repetitions of these dreams create wrong beliefs and attitudes in life and lead to depression or frustration and create worry about the unknown future.

B. Negative Thoughts

These thoughts are related to disadvantages of various events and loss as being perceived by the individual. Such thoughts increase toxic chemicals in our body. These are the impressions in our active memories, which are related to low self-esteem, inferiority complex, weak impressions, vicious habits and tendencies, selfishness, anger, ego and attached blind emotions. These impressions with very negative emotions even compel us to act without any decision of intellect. These negative emotions of our memories are very powerful. They incapacitate the intellect by creating mental limits, false associated assumptions, prejudiced judgments and hasty or blind actions. For example:

i. If any mistake happens, we often say, 'this is my nature, I can't help it, I have always been like that, I will not change now, it is too late...' thus we make a limit and create a comfort zone with these unnatural tendencies and these limits become a strong mental logical barrier in our subconcious mind that makes it impossible for us to find the solution of a problem.

ii. There may be someone regularly cleaning the office, where we have a set of beautiful flower vases of glass. By chance, he happens to break it. We cautioned him that he has to be careful otherwise must replace the same with another one if broken again. After a few days same thing happened as he was cleaning again and he broke another one. We became firm with him and told him the next time if he breaks anything; he has to replace it with another one from his own pocket. Some days later, we came to the office and as we passed by that place we found that the flower vase was broken and mended with some solutions. Whose name will come to our mind? Immediately we associated our previous memory and took the same person and took action against him but actually it was not him, it was somebody else who had done that. Thus, we see here that our own negative thoughts and emotions led us to a prejudiced wrong judgement.

iii. There is one more story, which explains how our negative emotions lead us to blind deadly actions. There was a farmer who had a mongoose as pet. The farmer and his son with this pet used to live together. Pet was very lovely and faithful. All of them lived and slept together. One day the farmer went outside leaving his son and pet at home. Suddenly, a cobra appeared and it was about to bite the farmer's son. Suddenly, the pet bounced and caught the snake and cut it into pieces. The pet fulfilled its loyalty to the farmer. Its mouth was full of blood. The farmer's son was afraid and had hidden himself in another room. When the farmer came back, the pet appeared before him proudly with more loving emotions expecting same from the farmer in lieu of its loyalty. But the farmer's conscious mind flooded with negative associated memories from the subconscious mind created strong negative emotions of hatred (thinking that the blood in the mouth of his pet was that of his son and his son is no more and his pet had killed his only son in his absence) and at once raised the spade kept in the corner of the room and killed his pet on the spot. After that his son appeared before him and by seeing his son he became dumbstuck. And when he listened the true story from his son about the pet, he became grief stricken and started burning mentally in the fire of agony and repentance.

Thus, our own negative belief or impression makes us unfaithful, doubtful, resentful, weak and creates strong impressions of low self esteem in the memory bank which further make our personality negative and thus a man is trapped in his own negative vicious cycle.

C. Necessary Thoughts

There are strong impressions of repeated routine actions in our active memory or subconscious mind. These are the thoughts related to necessary activities and daily routine. Such thoughts cannot be avoided completely. A desire in conscious mind for a routine work or knowledge activates the memory by which necessary thoughts automatically occupy our conscious mind and intellect and activate motor organs of our body to perform the task. It is related to the day-to-day routine work, professional job, career plans etc. For example the desire to go to office from home and back automatically activates our motor organs and all necessary turns are made automatically to reach the destination. Similarly, a desire to type something activates stored necessary memory and fingers get automatic instructions from the subconscious mind to type the detail as far as it can. Thus our habits and tastes are part of necessary thoughts of our active memory or subconscious mind.

D. Positive Thoughts

Thoughts related to success, health, peace, self-esteem, and direct or indirect advantages of every event are called positive thoughts. These are value-based thoughts, which have no selfish intentions, and we feel joy, peace, happiness and enthusiasm. These are not fully at active state. When these positive thoughts mix with the thoughts and desires created by sense organs it creates a joyful and peaceful state of mind which further make our attitudes very positive and creates a constructive vision and powerful actions which makes our impressions pure and positive in active memory. Thus positive thoughts generate energy and strength to cleanse further our active memory and get rid of negative and wasteful memories.

E. Pure Thoughts (Thoughts of Higher Consciousness)

The thoughts, which replace impure thoughts (waste & negative thoughts) are called pure thoughts, which have the power to purify our own impressions of memories. **Constant generation of pure thoughts not only purifies our own latencies, habits and instincts but purifies others' nature also.** Pure thoughts are strong seeds of positive personality. They not only help an individual to become socially adaptable but empower him to become socially effective also. He thus plays a crucial role in a society to start a changing process. He becomes the centre of revolution for a pure and ultra modern civilization with peace, purity and prosperity, which becomes the root of all civilizations of the world.

F. Elevated and Powerful Thoughts

Thoughts related to spirituality, yoga and self-consciousness are called elevated and powerful thoughts. **They reduce toxic chemicals from blood and increase health-promoting chemicals.** These are the most powerful seeds in human being's unconscious mind. When this seed is watered by powerful emotions, the tree of a divine personality starts germinating. When the tree grows, it becomes the living divine idol or perfect personality on this earth. Thus, the powerful thoughts purify the whole nature. The powerful thoughts occur in the absence of all other thoughts. The third eye gets completely activated with the powerful thought. Power of silence flows all around and miracle starts happening. Individual reaches to the acme of spirituality. What science cannot do, spirituality does it. This is the state of "self" or "soul" consciousness.

Thought: The Most Powerful Subtle Energy

A thought is the seed of all actions. It carries the most powerful subtle energy in potential form. It is just like uranium, which makes a nuclear bomb. When uranium disintegrates by chain reaction, the energy is released. In the same way, when the thought is bombarded by emotions, it releases its massive energy as happens in the case of nuclear chain reaction. When a powerful seed of thought is bombarded by powerful emotions, a strong vibration is created into the universe. Waste and negative thoughts are just like a nuclear waste, which create hazard in the eco system.

Emotions: The Force that Directs Thought Energy

Emotions give motion to thoughts' energy. It makes thoughts to move in the direction where emotions carry it further. It makes the being (soul) emotional by which, course of actions or reactions are determinated. Emotion is the force of determination too. That is why, a person is carried away by his emotions. It is also the marks that fit over deep true self and obscure us from ourselves. **Without emotion, thought is mechanical. Emotion makes**

the thought magnetic. Without emotion, thoughts can be compared to an engine running vehicle in a neutral gear. Emotion changes the gears of thoughts, which makes the vehicle of thought to move. Emotion can also be compared to involvement of heart and soul. Thought with emotion indicates involvement of mind's coordination with heart.

Thus emotion is the "Essence" or the prime source of motivation of the "Being". Performances and artwork were created with emotional energy only.

It can be easily understood by an example. Simply chanting mantra during prayer does not give peace of mind because it is mechanical at thought level. Prayer with divine emotions is called devotion. And devotion gives complete peace of mind, which activates our magnetic center that further creates effective and serene vibrations in the atmosphere.

Understanding one's own and others' emotions and taking empathetic view is called **"Emotional Intelligence".**

Types of Emotions

Emotions may be categorised as follow:

(a) *Positive Emotions:* Those emotions which create a positive state of mind and fill the mind with pure love, peace, bliss, joy and happiness etc. Following emotions are categorised as positive:

• pure love (true love)
• compassion
• peace or equanimity
• divine love (devotions) etc.
• laughter or mirth
• awe or wonder

(b) *Negative Emotions:* Negative emotions are afflictive and damaging to our goal of emotional harmony. These emotions fill the state of mind with fear, disgust, apprehension, anger, sex lust, pride etc. which further leads to depression and pessimistic attitude in life. Following emotions are categorised as negative emotions:

• erotic love or sex lust

- fear
- revulsion or disgust
- anger etc.

(c) *Powerful Emotions:* (Emotion of Valour and Heroism): Powerful emotion of valour and heroism fill our mind with courage and dynamism. They enable the modern day *Arjunas* to live their lives as **INTEGRATED BEINGS**, who don't allow its pressures and strains to fragment them. They mature into beings who, instead of running away, seek out their inner demons and dragons and face them bravely. They know they cannot control circumstances, but can responsed to them, and they go ahead and do precisely that. They don't let odds bog them down but seek out the courage, inner resources, and skills to advise, again and again, from the ashes of their old selves. Thus, the powerful emotions not only fill the mind with confidence and determination but germinate the powerful seed of thought also to rediscover the self with a perfect personality which becomes a catalyst agent for world transformation through self-transformation.

Effects of Thoughts and Emotions on the State of Mind and Body

Any thought in the conscious mind triggers respective emotional memory (good or bad) which in turn fills the mind with respective emotions (positive, negative or powerful), which further creates the respective attitude (positive or negative) which in turn triggers the intellect's vision to take respective decisions for actions which further creates, recreates or strengthens the impressions in our memory bank (sub-conscious mind), and these impressions stimulate the sensations (feeling) in our body by activating our endocrine glands. Thus any thought would follow the following path to affect our mind and body:

THOUGHTS >> EMOTIONS (FROM EMOTIONAL MEMORY) >> ATTITUDE >> VISIONS >> DECISIONS >> ACTIONS (BY BODY) >> IMPRESSIONS (IN MEMORY) >> SENSATION (FEELING IN BODY) OR REFLECTIONS >> ACTIVATION OF GLANDS AND RELEASING

TEAM OF CONSCIOUS MIND

T- Thoughts
E- Emotions
A- Attitude

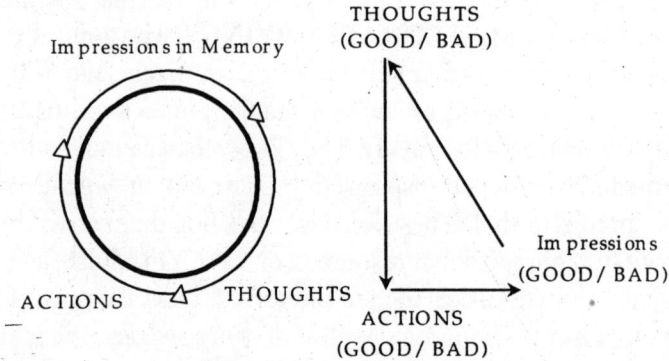

Impressions in Memory

ACTIONS   THOUGHTS

THOUGHTS
(GOOD / BAD)

Impressions
(GOOD / BAD)

ACTIONS
(GOOD / BAD)

M- Memories

Thoughts: It is the input in our conscious mind which either comes from perception by sense organs or automatically keeps coming from the memory bank (from subconscious or unconscious mind).

Emotions: When thoughts come from memories, they also carry emotions with it, which is also called **"emotional memory"**. Thus we can say that emotional memory is the memory attached to emotion in conjunction with past events, people and places. For example: you are driving a car with music on, suddenly an accident happens. Now this gets recorded in memory bank attached to the emotions or feelings while listening to that particular music during driving the car. Now, whenever you will listen that particular music, you will get the whole picture of the accident scene and your emotions will shift automatically.

The memory here indicates mental visual imagery (just like videotape or video CD, or DVD) of our past lives or past actions, reactions etc. It also contains some future planned images which are created by individual visualizations or we can say it is the imaginary world of the individual in which he expects or plans to live in. This is also known as *"unreal memory"*. When this file is opened in conscious mind, individual gets lost in the wild world of fantasies or imaginations. **Thus our memory bank contains real as well as unreal memories.**

Attitude (Thought + Emotions): When thought and emotions meet together, attitudes are created. Positive thoughts with positive emotions create positive attitude, negative thoughts with negative emotions create negative attitude. Thoughts without emotions create neutral attitude. A person with neutral attitude becomes sloth, careless and charmless.

In laymen's language "attitude can be described as intensity of emotion with thoughts" or "attitude indicates the magnitude of emotions with thoughts." In a more simple way it can be compared with an example: simple thought indicates a vehicle standing in the neutral gear of a running engine and attitude accelerates the vehicle by changing the gears (mode of mind).

Memories: Brain processing or memory accessing can be compared to separate filing cabinets:

A. Negative emotions record in memory bank

B. Positive emotions record in memory bank

AS ARE THE MEMORIES SO IS THE CONSCIOUSNESS.

TEAM: *"Team" indicates Thought + Emotions + Attitude + Memory* together form thoughts in our consciousness or in conscious mind. The term "consciousness" indicates here the memory linked thoughts with emotional memory, which fills the state of mind with emotions which is called emotional state of mind and further determines our attitude in particular situation or circumstances.

Thus the "TEAM" of conscious mind further determines the course of intellect (the third eye). As the "attitude", so is the "vision" of the third eye. As the "vision", so is the "decision" and "action". As the "action" so is the "strengthening" of "impressions" in the memories. And as the "impressions" so is the "sensation" or feeling or "realization".

Example: The recollection of consciousness of a dog having once bitten someone now fills the mind with the state of fear and attitude or mood (mode of mind) of aversion. He views the dog as an enemy and acts with a stick. This in turn strengthens the impression of fear from a dog in his subconscious mind (memory). Thus the feelings of a man depend upon what he is conscious of. This team will further affect our body.

How Do Our Mind and Body Get Affected by Team

Effects of Bad Team on Mind: Bad thoughts are Negative Emotions >> Negative Attitude >> Imperfect Visions (misconceptions) >> Wrong Decisions >> Hasty Actions >> Bad Impressions >> Feelings of Depression >> Mind Becomes Un-eased (Dis-eased) by anger, agitation and excitement etc.

Effect of Bad Team on Body by Anger : Releases bad cholesterol LDL (low density lipo proteins) >> Blocks heart vessels >> Blood pressure rises leading to heart attacks and intestines get wounded causing ulcers, etc.

Effect of Bad Team on Body by Agitation: Increases the activity of the sympathetic nervous system >> Increases pressure in the small blood vessels of the brain >> Brain vessels are ruptured leading either to brain hemorrhage or brain tumour/cancer.

Effect of Bad Team on Body by Excitement and Fear: Activates adrenal glands >> Negative harmones (adrenaline/cortisol) released >> Causes many disorders or disease in body organs such as diabetes, kidney failure, skin disease etc.

THUS A DISEASED TEAM LEADS TO A DISEASED BODY

Thought Attack Leads to Heart Attack

Thus, by above chain reaction of thoughts, it is quiet obvious that a waste or negative thought can lead to heart attack. Thus, the thought attacks are more deadly than heart attacks. It not only causes heart attack by paralysing the whole inner system of being but also paralyses our body.

Effects of Good Team On Mind: Good thoughts (positive, elevated and powerful thoughts) >> Positive emotions >> Positive attitude >> Creative and constructive vision of intellect >> Effective decision >> Successful action >> Remarkable impressions in memory >> True realization (feeling) of our own potential >> Thrilling and happy sensation in body >> Stability or easiness in mind, which further makes our body healthy.

Effects of Good Team On Body:

1. Creates balance between sympathetic and parasympathetic system, between steroid hormones and lactic acid, stabilises blood pressure to the necessary level and so on >> Healthy mind and receptive mind in a well nourished brain for better memory.

2. Releases endorphin and encephalin hormones >> Gives relaxation to 60 trillions of cells in human body >> Human system and organs remain healthy and disease free.

3. Releases HDL (High Density Lipo protein) i.e. good cholesterol >> Replaces bad cholesterol >> Blockage clearing of heart vessels >> Makes our heart filled with pure love and positive emotions >> Rules out chances of heart attacks.

Thus, a healthy TEAM leads to healthy body (a better place for being – the soul to live in).

How A Good Team Leads to Success

When we think positive in a happy and confident frame of mind, we easily get access to our subconscious impressions of successful experiences while presented with the problems. With a positive mood, we can recall all the successful solutions to the similar problems of the past, thus increasing our chances of a successful solution. When we are linked to impressions of negative emotions while facing a problem, our search for solution from our memory becomes a futile exercise because we keep accessing failure memories only from our experiences of the past.

How to Switch Over from Bad Team to A Good Team

To switch over from a bad team to a good team we have to create our own magic trigger. So select a magic trigger from the past successful memories. It has to be selected and practised well in advance. It cannot be set up when we are already in our negative mood due to our own bad team. Thus the magic trigger becomes a permanent key of positive experience. Now whenever you are in a sad or depressed mood due to your bad team, take the following five steps:

Step I : Recall the Magic Trigger,

Step II : Recall the scene of magic trigger in complete detail,

Step III : Feel the same emotions while replaying the actual event in detail,

Step IV : Now experience the change of mood and remain in the same feeling and experience for some time,

Step V : Now challenge the problem being faced and search for a solution. You will certainly find it.

●●●

4

SCIENCE OF MIND CONTROL

Science of Mind Control System by the Third Eye

The faculty by which the soul can select its desired thoughts and emotions is **INTELLECT,** which is also known as third eye or divine eye or the rational self. The expressions "will power" is often used to refer to our ability to put our ideals into practice. We know our well being and resist activity, which is harmful. This is directly related to soul's intellectual strength. When we speak of weakness or strength in the soul, we are referring to the intellect. In the case of a weak soul it is almost as if the intellect plays no part in determining which thoughts arise in the mind, but come as if pushed by the impressions of subconscious mind or are triggered by the atmosphere around or the moods of others. On the contrary, a powerful soul enjoys the experience of its own choice regardless of external stimuli. **Thus intellect performs three functions:**

(a) Analyse or discern or discriminate

(b) Visualise the several images related to the selected thoughts

(c) Judge or decide

In other words, we can say that the intellect is gifted by the soul with three powers:

(A) Power to **Discriminate**

(B) Power to **Visualise**

(C) Power to **Judge**

"THIRD EYE IS THE KEY OF MEMORY BANK"
Key Functions of the Intellect

Out of these three powers, **power to visualise** is the most.

important function of the intellect. **That is why, intellect is also known as the 'third eye' or 'eye of knowledge' and this is the eye of soul.**

Decision making, discernment or discrimination power, reasoning power, ability to remember, associate and identify, will power, ability to understand, know and recognise, judgement etc. are the **key functions of the rational self. Intellect, being the ruler of the mind, is the principal faculty of the soul.** The feeble and befuddled intellect subjugates itself to two worlds: one is the eternal world of senses, and the other is the internal world of thoughts, feelings and personal traits.

Intellect allows or refuses entry of thoughts into the process of action and result according to its own set of rules and perceptions that constitute our belief system which in turn control our attitudes. The accuracy of the role of intellect as doorkeeper can be heightened through meditation so that positive qualities are permitted while negative ones are weakened and transformed.

The strengths or weaknesses of an individual depends upon how efficiently the intellect functions. Some impressions are active, some are latent and some are inactive. **The third eye activates the latent and inactive impressions through the power of visualisation.**

Methods of Visualisations
(by third eye to control the mind and programme the memory)

Mental Movies Method: This is one of the best methods of visualisation for subconscious mind programming. Follow the following steps —

a. Relax yourself and sit down comfortably as you sit down to watch a movie in a theatre.

b. Immobilise your attention. Withdraw yourself from sensory perception. Feel happy that you are going to see the best movie of your choice.

c. Visualise a screen in front of you. Start making colourful mental pictures systematically and not randomly. It is better to form a systematic blue print of your mental movie.

d. During visualisation feel the true emotions as it is happening in real. Concentrate with all sensory perception that you are listening to the talks and feeling it very real and you are extremely happy for realising your goal in your life. You must act as if this is already an objective reality.

e. Remain in happy mood and feel you are repeating this story to your friends, parents etc and listening their voices and feeling excited and going to sleep. Your memory is programmed now. Wait patiently and start the systematic work as per your blue print and see the success is being realised without any hindrances.

Recovery of a Patient from Paralysis: A patient suffering from functional paralysis used to visualise a vivid picture (like movie) of himself walking around in his office, touching the desk, answering the telephone and doing all the things he ordinarily would do if he were healed. He repeated these visualisations exercise daily. By doing so he programmed his memory with the impression of perfect health. He continued this visualisation regularly. Then, one day the telephone rang at a time when everyone else was away. The telephone, was then a few feet away from his bed, nevertheless, he manages to answer it. His paralysis vanished from that hour on. **The healing power of his memory bank had responded to his third eye imagery, and a healing followed.**

This man had suffered from a mental block that prevented nerve impulses generated in the brain from reaching his legs. Therefore, he could not walk. When he shifted his attention to the healing power within, his power flowed through his focussed attention and he could walk again.

Alpha Mind Technique: Alpha mind means relaxed state of mind when there is absence of Beta activities in the brain waves. Brain waves remain in Alpha pattern with a frequency between 8 to 12 cycles per second (Hz). In this state, the negative thoughts, which tend to neutralize our desire and so prevent acceptance by our subconscious mind, are no longer present.

Alpha state of mind occurs during a drowsy state or sleepy state and after you have just woken up. Alpha state of mind can also be created by deep contemplation, relaxation techniques and meditation. In alpha mind techniques, a person visualises his suggestion, which easily gets impressed in our memory bank because our subconscious mind remains quite receptive due to absence of any conscious efforts or activities. Suppose you want to get rid of a destructive habit.

Assume a comfortable posture, relax your body, and be still. Slowly you will feel going into a sleepy state. During that time say quietly over and over, "I am completely free from my bad and destructive habits. I am a peaceful soul, I am a pure soul." Repeat these words slowly, quietly and lovingly with true feelings daily before going to bed and just after waking up in the morning. Each time with repetition the emotional value becomes greater. And later on when the urge comes to repeat the negative habit, repeat this formula out loud to yourself. Say, I am a pure soul. By this means you induce the memory bank to accept the idea and a healing follows. And efficacy of control system improves.

Prayer Method: To affirm is to state that it is so as you maintain this attitude of mind as true, regardless of all evidence to the contrary. You will receive an answer to your prayer. Your thoughts can only affirm, for even if you deny something. You are actually affirming the presence of what you deny. Repeating an affirmation, knowing what you are saying and why you are saying it, lead the mind to that state of consciousness where it accepts what you state as true.

Keep on affirming the truths of life until you get the subconscious reaction that satisfies. Never give up affirmation till you get the desired result. The effectiveness of an affirmation is determined largely by our understanding of the truth and meaning that underlie the words. The power of our affirmation lies in the intelligent application of definite and specific positive thoughts. Suppose a school child adds two and three and puts down four on the blackboard. The teacher affirms with mathematical certainty that two and three are five.

Therefore, the child changes the figure accordingly. The teacher's statement did not make two plus three equal to five. This was already a mathematical truth. That in turn caused the child to rearrange the figure on the black board. The result of the affirmative process of prayer depends on confirming to the principles of life, regardless of appearances. There is a principle of truth but none of dishonesty. There is a principle of intelligence but none of ignorance, there is a principle of health but none of disease and there is a principle of harmony and none of discord, and there is a principle of abundance and none of poverty.

Thus to affirm is to accept something as true, to live in the state of being it. As we sustain this mood, we shall experience the joy of the answered prayer. Successful prayer requires the following basic steps:

a. Acknowledge and admit the problem.
b. Drop the problem into the memory bank, which alone knows the most effective solution or way out by third eye.
c. Rest with a sense of deep conviction that it is done, visualise it confidently by your third eye.

These steps will enable the kinetic energy behind the prayer to takeover.

Logical Method: This method consists of spiritual reasoning. You have to convince yourself that the instability of mind, stresses in your mind or sickness are the result of false beliefs, groundless fears and negative pattern of impressions in the memories.

You have to reason it out clearly in your mind and convince that the diseases or ailments are due to only distorted and twisted patterns of thought that has taken form in the body.

This wrong belief in some external power and external causes have now externalised itself as sickness and can be changed by changing the thought patterns.

In this method, you explain logically to yourself or the sick person that the basis of all healing is a change of belief. You must convince him that healing powers are hidden in the memory bank. You have to logically argue through your intellect in the courtroom of your objective mind that disease is a shadow of the mind, which is based on disease soaked in morbid thought image. Memory bank has an impression of a perfect pattern of every cell, nerve, and tissue within it.

Then, you must render a verdict or judgement through your intellect in the courthouse of your mind in favour of yourself and your patience. You liberate the sick one by strong faith, firm belief and spiritual understandings. Your mental and spiritual evidence is overwhelming. Since there are hidden impressions, what you feel as true is manifested in the experience of yourself or the patient, and healing follows automatically.

Rajyoga **Method:** Many people throughout the world practise this form of treatment with wonderful results. I personally practised it during my treatment of cancer, diabetes and hepatitis-C. This method can be used to heal self and others too. In this method, you visualise yourself in your true form, you slowly shift yourself into soul consciousness, after that you silently think of God and His qualities and attributes, such as God is blissful, ocean of love, infinitely intelligent, all powerful, a source of boundless wisdom, absolute harmony, indescribable beauty and perfection. You quietly think and visualise along this lines, your consciousness is lifted into a new spiritual dimension. Your memory bank is opened. You get connected to the infinite intelligence. You feel the infinite ocean of God's love dissolving everything unlike itself in the mind and body.

You feel all the power and love of God are now focused on you and especially on the diseased organ of the body. Whatever is bothersome or vexing is now completely neutralised in the presence of the infinite ocean of love. Try to remain in this state of mind for quite some time. Healing has to follow, there is no doubt in it. After this you feel becoming completely all right and healthy.

You can heal others by this method also. You can visualise the patient and his diseased organ during this Rajyoga exercise. This method might be compared to the latest development in ultrasound, which generates powerful sound waves at extremely high frequencies. When these waves are focused on areas of the body where there are abnormal tissues, the affected cells resonate to the ultrasound and respond to it.

Similarly, to the degree, that we rise in consciousness by contemplating the qualities and attributes of God, we generate spiritual waves of harmony, health and peace. Those on whom these waves are focused, they resonate to them and respond. Many remarkable healings have been achieved by this technique of *Rajyoga*.

Additional Chief of Brahma Kumaris Dadi Janki practises this meditation and is a living example for all of us. She remains in delta stage of mind all the time, she has been described as "The most stable mind in the world" by the scientists at the University of Texas, America and "A woman of perfect rhythm" by Australian scientists. She generates strong spiritual waves of health, harmony and peace all the times and serves the world indirectly.

Blessing Method: A person who has practised Rajyoga for quite sometime can practise this method. Spiritual power goes into the world according to the feeling and faith behind it. When a Rajyogi realises the power, which moves the world, is moving on the spirit's behalf and is backing the word uttered mentally, his confidence and assurance grow. You do not try to add power to power. There must be no mental striving, coercion, force, or mental wrestling. You just visualise the decree strongly that goes with boundless love, and infinite power, which brings the decree to be realised. Thus, what you bless and feel as true will come to pass. Keep blessing the world with health, harmony, peace and abundance of love indirectly. This is the incognito part you can play for serving the world. You can become a saint by using this method.

Why Our Desires are not Fulfilled?

Doubts and hesitation only weaken our prayer. Don't say to yourself, "I wish I could be healed" or "I hope this works". Our feeling about the work to be done sets the tone. Harmony is ours and health is ours.

When our desires in conscious mind and visualisation by third eye are in conflict, our visualisation invariably gains the way.

Suppose, you were asked to walk along a narrow plank that

was resting on the floor. You would do it easily, without question. But now suppose the same plank were twenty feet up, stretching between these walls, would you walk it? You would probably not. Your desire to walk the length of the plank would come into conflict with your visualisation. You would visualise yourself toppling off the plank and falling along the way to the ground. You might very much want to walk across the plank, but your fear of falling would keep you away from being able to do it. The more effort you put into conquering your visualisation or suppressing it through your desire, the greater strength is given to the dominant visual imagery of falling.

Mental effort often leads to self-defeat, creating the opposite of what is desired. It is like deciding that you will do everything not to think of a black monkey. The decision makes the idea of a black monkey dominate the mind and our memory bank always responds more to the dominant idea. It will accept the stronger of the two contradictory propositions. May be you find yourself thinking:

- I want a healing, why can't I get it?
- I try so hard, why don't I get the result?
- I must force myself to pray harder.

Now you can realise where the error lies for the failure in fulfillment of your desires or prayers.

All these are due to mental pressures. Mental pressures raise your brain's beta activities and the door of memory bank gets automatically locked. And no idea can enter into your subconscious mind. Reflect on the following example:

Have you ever had something like this happen to you?

You have to take an examination of some kind. You have put in a lot of time studying and reviewing the material. You feel as if you know it well. But when you face a blank exam page due to not knowing certain question's answer, you find that your mind is even blanker. All your knowledge of the subject has suddenly deserted you. You can't recall a single relevant thought. You grit your teeth and summon all the power of your will but the harder you try, the farther the knowledge seems to flee.

All this happens due to rise in beta brain activities because of mental pressure. This further leads to the closure of memory bank. You get frustrated and leave the examination room. When the mental pressure eases and brain waves fall down to normal beta range, suddenly the answers you were hunting so desperately a few minutes ago flash suddenly into your mind. You told yourself that you know the material, and sure enough you did but not when you needed to. The mistake you made was "to force yourself to recollect". And this force or mental pressure leads to failure and what you got was the opposite of what you asked or prayed for.

Your failure to get the desired result may be the consequence of mentally making and visualising following of the few statements:

- Things are getting worse.
- I will never get an answer.
- I see no way out.
- It is hopeless.
- I don't know what to do.
- I am all mixed up. And so on.

When you use such statements, you get no response or cooperation from your hidden impressions of memory bank. Imagine that you got into a taxi and instructed the driver with a half dozen different directions. He would become hopelessly confused. He might refuse to take you anywhere. Even if he tried to follow your instructions, chances are that he would not be able to. Where you would end up is anybody's guess.

How to Fulfill Your Desires?

The act of visualising opposition creates opposition. If your attention is focused on the obstacles in obtaining what you desire, it is no longer concentrating on the means to obtain your desire. In this process, impressions of obstacles obstruct your desire not getting realised. Therefore, there must be harmonious union or agreement between the two faculties (Conscious mind and Intellect) of our objective mind to unlock and activate the powerful impression of subjective mind and to realise our dreams and prayers.

When there is no longer any quarrel between the different parts of our objective mind (Conscious mind and Intellect), our prayer will be answered. If you visualise the reality of the fulfilled desire and feel the thrill of accomplishment and where opposition is completely absent, your hidden impressions brings about the realisation of your desire.

Many great people solved all this dilemmas and problems by the play of their controlled, directed and disciplined visualisation by their third eye. They never visualised any opposition in their prayers but only affirmation in their prayer. They know whatever they visualise and feel sure that it will and must come to pass.

Affirmative prayers mobilise all the mental and spiritual law of our subconscious mind. Their law is true for good ideas, but it holds true for bad ideas as well. Consequently, if you use your hidden impressions negatively, it brings trouble, failure and confusion. When used constructively, it brings guidance, freedom and peace of mind.

•••

5

SCIENCE OF MEMORY

Now let us see the last system of self, "The Memory System" (Its faculties are Subconscious mind and Unconscious mind, which are called memory bank). **Impressions of every action, observation and imagination in Subconscious Mind and Unconscious mind are called Memory.**

The memory bank or the treasures of impressions are known as *"Sanskar"*. The Psychoanalysts say that it is the sleeping mind or involuntary mind or even female mind (because female controls the male now-a-days, similarly female mind controls the male mind that is conscious mind).

What is a Memory Bank?

It is our inner garden: This storehouse is also known as a garden. Soul is the gardener. As the soul plants the seeds of thoughts with the help of an implement known as intellect in the garden of subconscious mind, so shall it reap in the body of environment. Imagine your subconscious mind as a bed of rich soil that will help all kinds of seeds to sprout and flourish, whether good or bad. If you sow thorns, you will reap thorny plants and if you sow roses, there will flourish a rose garden in the body of environment. Every thought is a cause and every condition is an effect. This is the reason it is so essential that you take charge of your thoughts through enhanced power of third eye.

Begin now to sow thoughts of peace, happiness, right action, good will and prosperity. Think quietly and with conviction on these qualities. Continue to plant these wonderful seeds of thought in the garden of your subconscious mind and you will reap a glorious harvest. Once you begin to control your thought processes with the help of your intellect, you can apply the powers, which are hidden in your storehouse to solve any problem or difficulty.

If you repeatedly say to your memory bank, "I cannot do it," your memory will create the same environment in the body and mind and you will feel incapable of doing it.

It is like Software of Human Computer: Let us understand this with one more example. Your body is like a ship. You are the navigator of the ship. You navigate this ship with the computerised cabin devices. This cabin can be compared to the brain of the body. The software in these computerised devices are known as memory data. As you press the required button, so is the response from these devices, which create conditions for smooth navigation. Similarly, your memory bank receives order from you through conscious mind and intellect and it response accordingly through physical body for navigating life in the ocean of the world. Be sure, your subconscious mind follows only your orders. If you press the button of fear, worry and anxiety through the thought system of your conscious mind and visualise the same things through your third eye (the Intellect), your subconscious mind or memory banks will act accordingly and will activate fear syndrome in the physical body and the same will be reflected through the face which is also known as the index of the mind.

It is the Basis of Our Consciousness: Subconscious mind or Impressions *(sanskar)* is a major manifestation of human consciousness (soul). It can be compared to a receptacle that contains habits, tendencies, personality traits, memories, values, beliefs, learning, talents, instincts etc. The quality of activities of the other two manifestations of human soul i.e. mind and intellect are based on the quality of *sanskar* because it is the *"sansar"* (world) of our inner lives. It gives the soul its specific configuration, just as each compound has a specific chemical configuration, depending on which it reacts.

It is the Archives of All Previously Recorded

Experiences: It is the store of the complete data of the soul's roles in the entire life on this world stage and this is the basis of our individual uniqueness. Impressions (*Sanskar*), being the receptacle of original attributes, virtues, values and all the experiences, project thoughts, desires or feelings on the mind's screen initiating either positive or negative chain of awareness, thought, decision, action and experience depending on the state of soul consciousness or body consciousness respectively.

A thought, desire or feeling arises in human mind based on the past experiences recorded in memory bank.

It Influences Our Personality: There have been innumerable small and big events in the past, which have exerted their influences on our personality and have moulded our characters but which we do not often recognise consciously. Their influences lie in overt or dormant forms. These have become a part of our lives. Our present attitudes, beliefs, fears, prejudices and all that give us a pattern of unconscious or subconscious behaviour have been formed of these events. The negative experiences of the recent past get projected as negative thoughts, desires or feelings frequently because they are at the top of the stockpile of experiences in the receptacle of *sanskar*. Even our obsessions, our temper, our lifestyle is because of these. Some of these memories can perhaps be retrieved under special conditions or with the help of hypnotism or drugs. These implicit or latent memories determine, in part what we do and these influence us all the time.

It is this kind of memory to which Freud and psychiatrists of his school of thought give a very great significance. Comparing it to a glacier, which has 5/7th of its mass under water, these unconscious memories form a major part of one's personality and a forceful factor that influence its behaviour. These bear heavily on self. All brain-scientists, psychologists and psychiatrists agree that it is this, which gives continuity to one's personality. It is this unconscious memory, which gives a unified character or personality in man's normal state of wakefulness from moment to moment.

In Sanskrit language, these dispositions or unconscious memories, which are the result of previous actions, are called **impressions (*sanskars*)**. It is these, which give unity to the self.

The self coordinates the information received from various senses into various parts of the brain and gives to it an experimental unity without which the encoded memory would be meaningless.

Thus, when the conscious personality has its memories at subliminal or infraliminal level, it can be designated as "subconscious" or "unconscious mind".

It is the Seat of Long Term and Permanent Memory: Subconscious mind has the power to do anything on the basis of permanent information stored in it. It is the power of the subconscious mind that makes our heart to beat about 72 times per minute regularly for 60 to100 years. At any time, the subconscious mind is aware of many body functions including blood pressure, heartbeats, body temperature, chemical balances, blood flow, digestion, assimilation, taking care of emergencies etc. It is well known to psychologists that we can consciously be aware of only 7+2 or 7-2 items at a time. But our subconscious mind can be aware of a large number of items at a time for a longer period.

It is Not Under Our Conscious Control But Intellect Can Control it by The Power of Visualisation: The subconscious mind keeps controlling the function of heart, digestion, circulation, breathing etc. through eternally impressed processes, which are independent of conscious control. It accepts what is impressed upon it or what you consciously create by way of impression of new beliefs and ideas with the help of third eye. Subconscious mind does not reason things out as our intellect does. Intellect has the power to discriminate, judge and visualise a new idea, to make an impression in the subconscious mind to form a belief, but the subconscious mind acts only according to what is fed in it. Our subconscious mind is like a bed of soil that accepts any kind of seeds good or bad. Our thoughts are seeds. Sub- conscious mind never engages in proving whether these thoughts are good or bad,

Science of Mind Simplified

true or false. It only responds according to the nature of our thoughts and suggestions impressed through third eye.

The power of visualisation is the basis of **mind programming**. Mind programming means that if we can put information in a person's subconscious mind through his third eye, we can modify the person's behaviour. Conscious mind alone cannot put the information without the help of intellect in the subconscious mind.

Self-Awareness and Practice of Rajyoga can Dig Out Virtues from Our Memory Bank: Through the practice of soul consciousness and Rajyoga we will be able to dig out the original attributes of the soul from the bottom of the stockpile in the receptacle of sanskar. Thus, the positive chain of awareness – thought decision – action and experience get repeated every time we practise Rajyoga. With continued practice of Rajyoga, the receptacle of *sanskar* gets filled with positive experience of the original attributes, virtues and values. **With this change in self, the world changes.**

The Subconscious Mind can be Programmed Through Hypnotic Suggestions: A skilled hypnotist may suggest to one of his students in the hypnotic state that her back itches, to another that his nose is bleeding, to another that she is a marble statue, to another that she is freezing and the temperature is below zero. Each one will follow out the line of his particular suggestion totally oblivious to all those surroundings that do not pertain to the hypnotic suggestion.

Types of Impressons in Memory Bank

Following types of impressions are there in the Records of our Memory bank (Subconscious/unconscious mind).

(1) Impressions of the Standard Mind - Body Mechanism (Standard Files of Memory Bank)

* Regulation of heartbeat, blood circulation, pulse rate, respiration, maintaining body temperature, standard secretion of hormones and enzymes, maintaining normal biochemistry of blood, digestion, assimilation (transmitting food into tissue, blood muscles, bones etc.) and controlling of all vital functions.

It starts working automatically from autonomous nervous system functioning (involuntary actions) from the day the soul enters into a human body. No one teaches it. It is an inbuilt mechanism within the memory of the soul, which functions without a remote control and round the clock whether we are awake or sleep.

- All basic qualities (primary virtues) of a soul or spirit that is of knowledge, peace, purity, love, joy, bliss power and secondary virtues such as harmony, honesty, maturity, politeness etc.
- Vast source of our ideals, aspirations and altruistic urges.
- Solutions of all problems, vast information about creativity, art, science and everything. It has infinite intelligence and boundless wisdom.
- It has secrets of universe and infinite potential, which can do miracle.
- It is also known as **sixth sense or intuitive mind.**
- All spiritual powers, higher consciousness and supra consciousness.

(2) Impressions of Routine Work (Routine Files of Memory Bank)

- Information related to daily routine work, or day-to-day activities.
- Professional knowledge, skills and general informations of day-to-day affairs.
- Images of many persons and personality with whom we interact.
- Present identity, knowledge of music of own choice, various arts, cultures and customs etc.
- Vivid scenes of past happy moments and future realistic plans.
- Day to day information acquired by self-study, and through electronic and print media.
- Sad moments of past incidents or accidents, future fantasies, future apprehensions, anxieties and fears (false evidences appearing real).

(3) Impressions of Past Events and Future Fantasies (Waste Files of Memory Bank)

- Vivid scenes of past sad moments and accidents.
- Images of future unrealistic plan and fantasies or unrealistic daydreams.
- Impressions of vicious acts like lust, greed, anger, ego, attachment etc.
- Unrealistic images which lead to apprehensions, worry, anxiety, fears, depression etc.
- Under confidence and inferiority complex and low syndrome (laziness, procrastination, frustration and pessimistic approach of life).
- Irritative tendencies

(4) Impressions of Negative Traits and Habits (Negative Files of Memory Bank)

- Images of habitual offences and vicious scenes impressed upon memory either due to continuous visualisation of imaginary vicious acts, by reading pornographic materials or continuous watching sinful acts in movies or TV serials or video CD, MMS clips etc.
- Images of porn pictures, which creates intense negative emotions for vicious acts and violence.
- Impressions of negative behaviour, reactive tendencies, humiliating incidents, or revengeful ideas etc., which fuel negative emotions to commit crime.
- Images of ego, lust, greed, jealousy, hatred etc.
- Impressions of negative propaganda or suggestions by family, friends, public or media, which cause distress and depression.

Subconscious and Unconscious Mind are like VCD/ DVD player, Conscious mind is like screen and Intellect is the eye of soul: Conscious mind is the screen of human beings' computer. Subconscious mind is the VCD or DVD player which automatically keeps playing various VCD/DVD, sending many images of various fields on to the screen of conscious mind and through intellect (the third eye), the soul keeps on viewing these images and data selects it, discriminates it, judges it and orders the motor organs of the body to execute the decisions and feels accordingly.

Thus whatever thoughts, beliefs, opinions, theories or claims we write, engrave or impress on our subconscious mind, we will experience them as the objective manifestations of circumstances, conditions and events. What we write on the inside, we will feel or experience on the outside. Thus, we have two sides of our life – objective and subjective, visible and invisible, thoughts and its manifestations.

If you click on negative files of subconscious mind and think negatively, destructively, and viciously; these thoughts generate destructive emotions and these negative emotions interfere with standard function of involuntary system and thus cause diseases in the body like heart trouble, hypertension, anxieties etc. And again these worries, anxieties, fear, and depression interfere with the normal functioning of the heart, lungs, stomach and intestines. Thus, it becomes a vicious circle because these negative patterns of thoughts keep interfering with the harmonious functioning of standard system of our subconscious mind. The law of action and reaction is universal. Our thoughts are the actions and reactions are the automatic response of our subconscious mind to our thoughts.

Therefore, keep your objective mind busy with the expectations of the best, and your subconscious mind will faithfully reproduce your habitual thinking. Visualise the happy ending or solutions to your problems and feel the thrill of accomplishment.

Laws of Memory Bank

Our memory bank is automatically governed by a set of laws. We must know that laws make changes in our lives style. These laws are as follows:

Law of Belief: The belief of our mind is the strong impressions of thoughts visualised by the third eye or seen by the two eyes of physical body and experienced it to be true. Belief does not mean faith in the same ritual, ceremony, form, and institution or formula, it is talking about belief itself – simply thought of our mind.

All our experiences, events, conditions and acts, which are reproduced by our memory bank, are the reactions to our thoughts, with which we trigger it. A firm belief activates the hidden potential of memory bank to bring about the result.

A thought is an input in our conscious mind, which acts as memory trigger, or incipient action and the reaction is the response from our memory bank that corresponds to the nature of our thoughts, which entered into our memory bank.

Thus, our memory bank acts like an ATM machine. As you press the button so is the response from the machine. **Fill your bank (ATM Machine) with the concept of harmony, health, peace, goodwill, eternal varities and truths of life and wonders will happen in your life and you will move onward, upward and Godward.**

You will get what your memory bank is filled with.

Stop filling your memory bank with the false belief, wrong opinions, superstitions and fears, which has plagued the human kind.

Law of Self-Preservation: Impressions of natural instincts preserve our physical body by constant renewal processes.

In almost eleven month our whole physical body is changed. Our stomach lining is replaced every five days. Our skin gets replaced once a month, our skeleton in every three months, even the DNA which holds the genetic material holding memories of millions of years of evolutionary time, the actual raw material of DNA, the carbon, the hydrogen, the nitrogen – comes and goes every six weeks like migratory birds. Our physical body of two years ago is dead and gone and this is the clinching proof of soul's self-preservation and also a proof of a "LIFE AFTER DEATH".

We are riding these molecules of body but we are not the molecules we ride. This skin comes and goes every month. It reincarnates once a month, but it does not forget to give the feeling of pleasure and pain. Our stomach cells change every five days, but they do not forget how to make hydrochloric acid as they incarnate and reincarnate every five days. With the above example it is quite obvious that we are not our physical bodies but we are riding our physical bodies with inbuilt impressions of self-preservation instincts in our memory bank or subconscious mind which keep functioning automatically without the knowledge of our conscious mind and intellect.

The Greek philosopher Herculite has rightly said that you should think of the human body as something like a river. Just like you cannot step into the same river twice because the new water is flowing in, similarly the real you (soul) cannot step into the same flesh and bones twice.

This is proved scientifically. When we breathe in and out we breathe in 1022 atoms from every where else and every time we breathe out 1022 atoms. And these atoms have their origin in every cells of our body. So at the atomic level we are sharing our organs with each other.

Law of Substitution: According to the law of substitution, you can activate the impressions of the joy of freedom by your third eye, which can recondition your memory bank. If you have activated the impressions of negative thoughts and conditioned your memory bank negatively, you could also activate the impressions of positive thoughts and recondition your memory positively by the law of substitution of your memory bank.

If your third eye took you to wrong habits and stressed life, it now can take you to freedom and peace of mind too. By the law of substitution, you visualise the images of freedom, sobriety and perfection and feel the thrill of accomplishment. When fear knocks the door of the mind, let faith in God and all good things substitute the fear. **By the law of substitution only, you can get rid of bad habits and negative thought patterns.**

Law of Concentrated Attention or Visualisation: According to this law the idea or any scene that realises itself is the one to which we give the most concentrated attention or visualise vividly.

Due to concentration or more attention on thoughts or ideas by our objective mind, the related impressions of memories get quickly activated and realised in practical life. These are the powerful thoughts or ideas, which are enveloped with the power of emotion to get quickly visualised and realised by our subconscious mind. When you are most attentive, to the idea of failure, it is failure that the subconscious mind brings into reality. The fear of failure itself creates the experience of failure by the law of concentration.

If you concentrate on confidence, courage and power, your memory bank will reflect the same. Whatever be your mental picture of attention or concentration, your subconscious mind will bring it to happen as per the law of concentration.

Law of Compulsion: Repeating the thoughts or repeating the acts over a period of time from active impressions in memory bank.

After that it becomes a second nature apart from our natural nature (first nature), which becomes a habit. Later on, the human being gets placed under the compulsion of a habit.

This is known as the law of compulsion. If you repeat a negative thought and keep drinking or smoking or doing any bad habits regularly over a period of time, you will place yourself under the compulsion of these negative thoughts and habits. You will have the temptation of doing it automatically according to the law of compulsion. That is why people feel incapable of giving up their bad habits or negative thoughts and emotions, which are hunting their mind with fear, worry and anxiety.

The active impressions of bad habits and negative thoughts start interfering the state of mind under the law of compulsion despite our mental effort or mental coercion against the bad habits. This leads further to frustration, depression and mental paranoia. Law of compulsion of our memory bank makes our destructive habit to operate automatically like involuntarily action.

Law of Observation: If we observe any event or scene with involvement of all sense organs, it gets registered as it is seen. That is why, we remember our childhood so vividly. In childhood, there are no negative or waste thoughts, therefore the impressions of childhood remains forever and a child is called the father of the man. With the power of observations we can register anything in our memory for a longer duration.

Law of Memory Languages: As our computer has got programming languages, similarly our human computer has also got unique languages for mind programming. Only these languages get registered in our memory bank. If we want to improve our memory power, we must communicate with our memory bank in these languages only.

The following four types of languages programme our minds:

(1) **Image:** Image of any thing automatically get impressed in our memory. That is why, we recollect the faces of any previously seen person but unable to recollect the name.

(2) **Music:** Music too gets impressed automatically in our memory, but lyrics do not get impressed. That is why we feel more relaxed when we listen the music or do humming with music. Alpha music relaxes all muscle and cells of the body.

(3) **Colour:** Colour is also the language of mind. That is why, colourful things attract our attention and register the impressions of the things in our memory. Visualisation of colours not only tunes our inner body (energy body) but also removes the body pains, backache and muscle pain. For that reason only, infrared rays (heat therapy) are given during physiotherapy exercise to remove the muscle pain. Visualisation of "red" colour and pinpointing the energy of red colour to the pain affected region gives more relaxation and relief.

(4) **Art:** Art is the creativity of mind, which easily gets impressed in memory. That is why any movie, TV serials or any advertisement (Creative Arts) creates lasting impressions in our memory. **Rajyoga meditation is a mental art used for reconditioning and de-conditioning of our memory.**

•••

6

MIND AND BRAIN
RELATIONSHIP

Mind and Brain Relationship

When Albert Einstein died, his brain was brought in a laboratory and was examined meticulously and was compared with a common man's brain. On comparison it was found that there existed no dissimilarities of even .001 %. Both the brains were exactly similar. Then what made Albert Einstein's brain so special? It was the Einstein being's mind, which utilised more than ten percent of his brain's trillions of neurons.

Here mind means metaphysical or subtle organ of self, which uses physical brain either for logic, reasoning, and analysis or for art and creativity.

The human brain is a paired organ; it is composed of two halves, called cerebral hemisphere. The theory of the structure and functions of the mind suggests that the two sides of the brain control two different modes of thinking.

Just stop to wonder for a moment, how a two year old baby can master the task of speaking so effortlessly while most adult efforts at learning a foreign language tend to end up as more effort and less learning. Most children are born with right hemisphere dominant, when an infant learns a language; she does so with all her sense of smell, sounds, colours, feelings in the learning process. As we grow older, the left hemisphere modes of thinking which rely heavily on partial processes (without visualisations) of the intellect – logic, sequence, organisation – becomes dominant.

In the Zen tradition, the left mind is associated with the process of thinking and the right mind is associated with knowing. Most individuals tend to have a distinct preference for one or the other side of the brain. From very early in life, school and society too conspire to identify individual as the one or the other – arts or the science and label them as "creative or logical"

Mind uses left hemisphere of the brain for logical and verbal reasoning. It deals with words, analysis (breaking a part) and sequential thinking.

Mind uses right hemisphere of the brain for intuition, creativity, dealing with pictures, synthesis (putting together) and holistic thinking.

Brain itself does not do anything. In the absence of mind (conscious life force) brain is called dead.

Right hemisphere of the brain is mostly used by intellect's for creative and visualisation power (third eye).

Difference Between Mind and Brain

MIND	BRAIN
METAPHYSICAL (FACULTY OF THE SOUL)	PHYSICAL (PART OF BODY)
MINDS THOUGHTS ARE LIKE SOFTWARE	IT IS LIKE HARDWARE OF COMPUTER
THREE FACULTIES (MIND, INTELECT & IMPRESSIONS)	TWO PARTS OF BRAIN (LEFT AND RIGHT)
	LEFT IS USED FOR ANALYSIS RIGHT IS USED FOR CREATIVITY

THOUGHT AND EMOTIONS OF THE MIND (Subconscious, Conscious and Intellect) CREATE CYCLES OF WAVES IN THE BRAIN, WHICH ARE CALLED "BRAIN WAVES" AND THESE BRAIN WAVES ARE MEASURED BY ELECTRO ENCEPHALO GRAM (EEG).

Science of Mind Simplified

Types of Brain Waves

Thought is an energy, which is created in the conscious mind by the input of either sense organs or memories. When thoughts enter into the brain, brain waves are created. Thoughts can be compared to stones or pebbles and brain can be compared to a pond. When pebbles or stones of thoughts are thrown into the

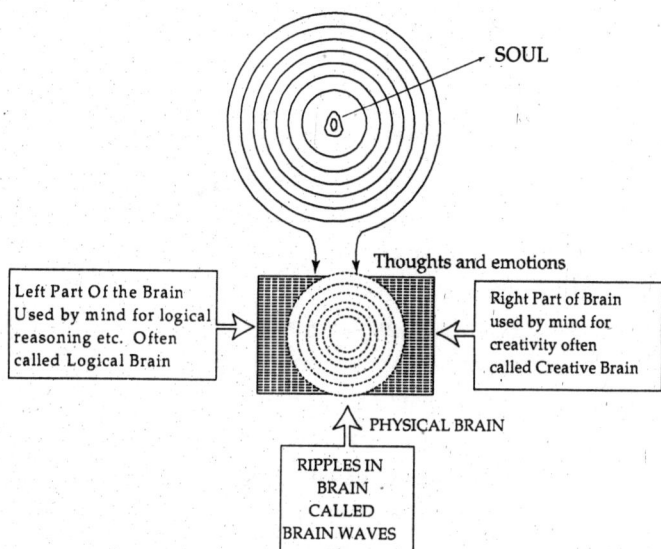

SOUL

Thoughts and emotions

Left Part Of the Brain Used by mind for logical reasoning etc. Often called Logical Brain

Right Part of Brain used by mind for creativity often called Creative Brain

PHYSICAL BRAIN

RIPPLES IN BRAIN CALLED BRAIN WAVES

pond of brain, ripples in the brain are created. Thoughts are also similar to electrical current. When an electrical current enters into a wire, a wave of frequency 50hz is created in the wire. These waves are categorised as per their frequency and voltage. These are:

(a) Alpha Waves: These are moderately fast (8 to 13 cycles per sec) and are relatively high voltage waves. Normally, EEG records these waves when an individual is awake, has his eyes closed and is in a relaxed state and his cerebrum is idling so to say. It keeps our mind and body in a relaxed and receptive state. It is having a vast potential for performance. Alpha state of mind triggers our standard impressions of memory.

(b) Beta Waves: These are comparatively faster (13 to 25 cycles per sec) than alpha waves but in amplitude they are lower in voltage. Beta waves are obtained when an individual is awake, has his eyes open, and is in an activated or attentive state, that is to say, when his cerebrum is not idling but is busily engaged with sensory stimulation and mental stimulation. Beta waves are further categorised as follows:

(1) *Normal Range*: Between 13 and 18 Hz. This is triggered by routine impressions. In this state we are busy and active. **Biochemistry, hormones and enzymes level remain within normal range.** Continuing in beta waves gives tiredness signal to subconscious mind.

(2) *Abnormal Range* (β+): Between 18 and 25 Hz. Thoughts of waste impressions of our memory bank trigger these waves. **Biochemistry and secretion of hormones and enzymes get affected.** Tiredness and stress increases. Disturbance in easiness of mind causes diseases in body.

(3) *Most Abnormal Range* (Super β): Between 25 and 50 Hz. Thoughts of negative impressions of our memory bank trigger these waves and further cause distress and depressions in life. **All types of diseases start, immune system gets weakened. Brain cells and capillaries get ruptured which further cause brain hemorrhage and paralysis.**

(4) *Deranged Range Beyond 50hz:* Sign of mental disorder and madness. It also indicates loss of memory.

(c) **Theta Waves:** These are moderately slow (3 to 7cycles per sec) and low voltage waves that predominate when drowsiness descends. This is a dream state. Consciousness never functions but intellect keeps functioning with uncontrolled visualisation of images from the subconscious mind.

All randomly recorded images (recorded by electronic or print media and by visualisations of waste and negative images during awake state) get opened during our dream state, which makes our brain to work during sleep. This lowers the potential and creates a low voltage. This further gives tiredness despite sleeping more.

(d) **Delta Waves :** These are the lowest (0.5 to 3 cycles per sec) brain waves and they have a high voltage. They are recorded when an individual is in deep sleep. Because of this fact, the physiologists refer to deep sleep as Slow Wave Sleep (SWS). This is the deep state of sleep that gives complete relaxation to our mind, intellect and body. Our mind and body get charged due to deep relaxation. Constant state of delta waves triggers our standard impressions, which renew us physically, mentally and spiritually. All inventions take place during this concentrated state of mind. **Mystery of universe sometimes gets revealed during dream waves between 3.5 to 4 Hz. If the EEG indicates that the cerebrum is producing no brain waves, it is called a flat EEG and is considered to imply that the individual is dead.**

These brain waves can also be understood by following examples: Brain is just like a pond, where water is still and one can see one's face very clearly as there are no ripples on the surface of water. Thoughts and emotions can be compared to pebbles and stones, when these pebbles and stones are thrown into the pond there are several ripples created on the surface of the water due to agitations caused by the stones. Similarly, when pebbles and stones of thoughts and emotions from our metaphysical mind enter into the pond of physical brain, agitations into the brain are caused and different types of brain waves are created depending upon the nature of (size of) pebbles and stones of thoughts and emotions from mind entering into the brain. One cycle in one second is called one Hz.

1 Cycle per second = 1 HZ
(FREQUENCY OF THE BRAIN IS MEASURED IN HERTZ)

Thoughts, Brain Waves and Body Relationshp

Thoughts of our mind create waves in our brain. These brain waves affect our endocrine system, which further change biochemistry of our body. The following table explains it in a simple way.

TABLE SHOWING THOUGHTS, BRAIN WAVES AND BODY RELATIONSHIP

Type of Thoughts	Comparison of size with pebbles or stones	Waves created in Brain by Thoughts & Voltage	Effects of Thoughts on Body
Negative	Very Big Stones	Very high Beta Waves(<than 25 Htz.) very low Voltage. Since energy comes out rapidly from body.	Distress state that causes BP & secretion of Adrenaline & Cortisol harmone, & biochemistry of the body is derailed & state of mind is fully disturbed.
Waste	Big Stones	High Beta waves. (more than 18 Htz.) Low Voltage because energy comes out due to repeated thinking.	Stressful state of mind, anxiety, fear, depression & Frustration. Low energy level. biochemistry of the body is disturbed. Digestive systems & endocrine system suffers.
Necessary	Small Stones	Beta waves. (up to 18 Htz.) & low voltage.	Normal state but apprehensive hasty decision & action, feels tired often.
Positive	Small Stress	Alpha Waves & High Voltage	Revised state of mind, Energetic, high voltage, dynamic state within. Ready to face any challenges in life, secretion of endorphin & encephelin gives relaxation to the whole body.
Dream stage (Random recorded thoughts coming From intellect automatically for imgination)	Small pebbles & stones	Theta waves &low voltage because energy comes out of body during imagination n the dreams.	Feels the reality as per imagination in dreams & the body reacts as it reacts during awake. i.e. Horror dream activies horror syndromes and the body reacts accordingly.
Deep Sleep State	Smallest pebbles	Delta waves &very high voltage energy remain present in the body	Completely relax state of mind as well as body. Balanced secretion of harmones & digestive juices. Full relaxation & very high degree of potential energy.

Extreme negative thoughts cause deranged range of brain waves beyond 50hz, which is a sign of mental disorder and madness. It also indicates loss of memory.

7

SOUL, MIND, BRAIN AND BODY RELATIONSHIP

Hypothalamus is that part of the brain which through the pituitary gland controls all the endocrine glands and the secretion of harmones and it also controls the state of awakening and sleep in conjunction with the RAS (Reticular Activating System) and acts for expression or inhibition of emotions in co-ordination with the thalamus and the limbic system and works for sense perception and other mental actions.

SEATED HERE ON A THRONE LOCATED AT A PLACE BETWEEN THE TWO EYEBROWS THE SOUL ACTS THROUGH THE MECHANISM OF THE BRAIN AND THE BODY.

The schematic drawing on next page shows the inter action of the mind and body and the sequence of stimulus and response.

Some neuro-scientists say that there is time-lapse of a couple of seconds (or even a split second) between the sensory message perceived (stage 4) and the triggering of the action (stage 6) onwards and thus we can conclude that at stage 5 the decision to do or not to do or how and when to do is taken and therefore this is what explains the existence of soul here.

This is the place of *"AKAL TAKHT"* from where the timeless soul rules the metropolitan city; called 'the body' it is the window from which the soul sees the world. It is the safety valve or the casket in which the soul, the greatest of all the treasures lies. Soul is the highest executive running and organising the most complex system known.

Though the soul is not a spatio-temporal entity and being infinitesimal, need not be pin-pointed in the brain, yet by indicating the place of its interaction with body mechanism, we can show

How soul acts through the mind and the body?

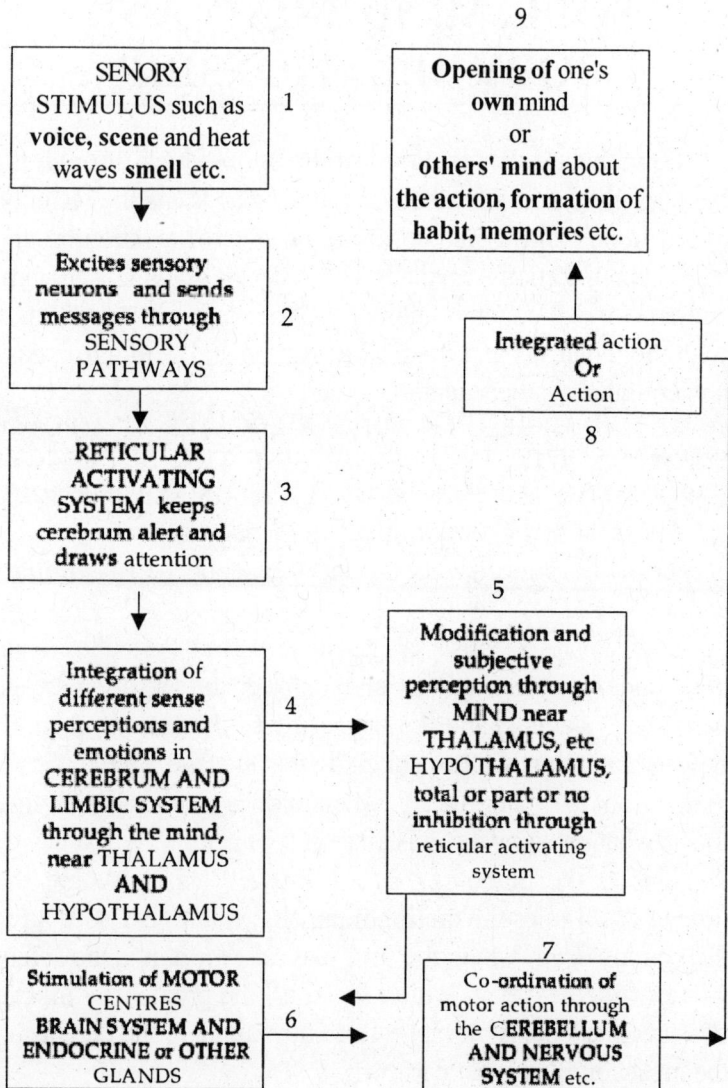

SENORY STIMULUS such as voice, scene and heat waves smell etc.	1	9 — Opening of one's own mind or others' mind about the action, formation of habit, memories etc.
↓		↑
Excites sensory neurons and sends messages through SENSORY PATHWAYS	2	Integrated action Or Action
↓		8
RETICULAR ACTIVATING SYSTEM keeps cerebrum alert and draws attention	3	
↓		5 — Modification and subjective perception through MIND near THALAMUS, etc HYPOTHALAMUS, total or part or no inhibition through reticular activating system
Integration of different sense perceptions and emotions in CEREBRUM AND LIMBIC SYSTEM through the mind, near THALAMUS AND HYPOTHALAMUS	4 →	
Stimulation of MOTOR CENTRES BRAIN SYSTEM AND ENDOCRINE or OTHER GLANDS	6 ← →	7 — Co-ordination of motor action through the CEREBELLUM AND NERVOUS SYSTEM etc.

Science of Mind Simplified

that the soul exists, that the soul is not identical with or omnipresent in the body but it acts through a control system and that it is not located in the heart muscle but in the heart of the brain which controls heartbeat and from here it acts through the body.

(Here Mind indicates all faculties of soul that is conscious mind, intellect and memory bank)

Correction of Wrong Data by Mind

Moreover, when it is found that the memory stored in the brain is wrong, it is the objective mind, which corrects it. For example, when certain lines of a poem have been wrongly learnt, or wrongly spelt, the mind after consulting the dictionary, decides to correct the stored information.

Thus the objective mind plays on the brain, which is another entity apart from it. There is give and take between the two. Not only are the memory banks at the disposal of the mind for being read or used but also the mind, by using of its ability or scrutiny, imagination or judgement, modifies the memories and moulds the memory-circuits.

•••

8

STRESS AND DISTRESS

Stress is an unavoidable consequence of life. Everyone at some point of time in his life faces situations where one has to make a choice. An adolescent who wants to choose the best career option suitable for his personality type, an adult who is soon to get married, a parent facing the problem of teenagers, an aged person who is depressed due to prolonged illness etc. are only some instances of stress. But there is no single level of stress that is optimal for all people.

Studies have shown that emotional factors, mental upsets and psychological maladjustments are repeatedly the cause of airplane accidents. The ability to think clearly and act decisively is greatly influenced by feelings and emotions.

In fact, every individual will panic earlier than the normal if he is suffering from fatigue, illness, worry or anger. But, even well away from the panic threshold, good judgement is seriously impaired under stress.

It has been found that most illnesses are related to unrelieved stress. **Unrelieved stress can lead to more serious consequences when faced by aircrew, who have to make split second decisions and a marginal decline in concentration and performance can be fatal.** Stress could be caused by a number of factors. It is very important to identify and treat them accordingly.

What is Stress?

Stress is an internal state of mind which can be caused by physical demands on the body or by mental drives or urges or by environmental and social situations which are evaluated as potentially harmful, uncontrollable and exceeding our resources for coping. Stress can also be defined as a mentally or emotionally disruptive condition that occurs in response to adverse external influences and is capable of affecting one's physical health, usually characterised by increased heart rate, a rise in blood pressure, irritability and depression. A person in a physically or mentally demanding situation is said to be under stress.

Stress is a form of pain, a messenger that comes from inside, which tells you that there is something, you need to learn and change. Stress is any external or internal situation that has harmful effects on the mind and body.

Pressures on Mind
Resilience Power

Stress is more if pressure on the mind is more and RP (Resilience Power) is less. The maximum stress is called distress. Stress is less if pressure on mind is less and RP is high. If pressure < Resilience power, it is called Marginal stress and Eu-stress.
If pressure > Resilience power, it is called stressed state and distress.
If pressure = Resilience power, it is called optimum stress.

(Here resilience power indicates 8 fold powers that is Power to Discriminate right or wrong, Power to Judge, Power to Face, Power to Adjust, Power to Tolerate, Power to Co-operate, Power to Pack-up (to be ever-ready for any work), Power to Withdraw from sense organs and just remain in the state of being, that is – peaceful, lovable, blissful, powerful, knowledgeful, joyful and pure.)

Types of Stress

There is no rule to classify stress but stress can be classified into the following categories –

Marginal stress: This is a state of insignificant stress where there is no burden or responsibility and an individual remains either in boring state or feel dejected. This is a state where an individual does not get any chance to prove his hidden potential and his performance level is undermined. His empty mind becomes a devil's workshop. He passes his time in non-productive activities.

Eu-stress: Eu-stress is positive and productive because it motivates and drives people to act and achieve their goals. It is also known as positive stress, which adds anticipation and excitement to life and we all thrive under a certain amount of stress.

Optimal stress: It is a state of stress where individual remains active and delivers his best. His performance level is hundred percent of his true potential. He has the power to face any challenge in his life. Optimal stress motivates but does not overwhelms us. For example competitions, confrontations and even frustrations and sorrow add depth and enrichment to our lives. There is no fixed criterion for optimal stress. It differs from man to man. It depends upon individual's knowledge and skill and his emotional and spiritual quotient.

Stressed state: This state is beyond optimal stress where individual feels burdened beyond his capability and develops a sense of being stressed with a lot of workload. This feeling reduces his handling capability of a situation and his hidden potential remains dormant. His performance level declines rapidly.

Distress: Distress reduces concentration and clear thinking. It may leave us feeling "tied up in knots". Distressing situations depend on our physiological and psychological responses to it. In this state, a person feels completely outwitted and insecured. If this situation persists for long, it may lead to mental breakdown.

In aviation, most activities require split-second correct decision and concentration to deal with emergencies. Flying fitness is not just a physical condition; it has a definite meaning in the psychological sense as well. It involves the ability of the pilot to perceive, think and act to the best of this ability without the hindering effects of anger, worry and anxiety.

The following graph explains **marginal stress, Eu-stress, optimal stress, stressed state** and **Distress**: -

GRAPH SHOWING VARIOUS LEVEL OF STRESS AND RELATED PERFORMANCE LEVEL

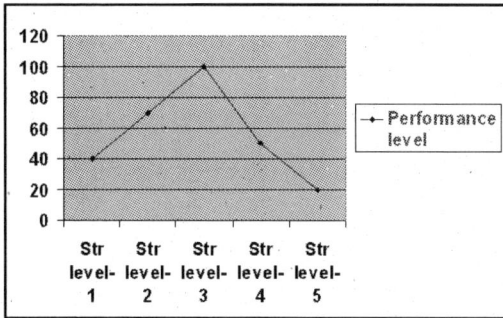

Stress level – 1 is insufficient stress or marginal stress, which acts as a depressant and may leave individual with feeling of getting bored or dejected and the performance level is just 40 %.

Stress level – 2 indicates eu-stress where performance level is 70% and a person strives to better his performance despite stress.

Stress level – 3 is the optimum level stress where performance level is 100%. Therefore, stress level 2 and 3 are also known as positive stress, which motivate individual to deliver his best performance.

Stress level – 4 indicates stressed state where performance level declines to 50% and a feeling of being stressed occupies the mind. The state of mind remains tensed. **It leads to a state of hypochondriasis.**

Stress level – 5 is a distress phase where an individual feels helpless, hapless and outwitted to unable to do his best and remains tied up in knots and his performance level declines drastically. **This is the most critical stage, which leads to fatal consequences in life.**

●●●

9

CAUSES OF STRESS (STRESSORS)

Causes of Stress

There are many factors that contribute to stress. Main causes of stress and distress in life are the presence of excessive pressure of waste and negative thoughts, wrong values, wrong belief systems, wrong opinions and the countless questions (what, why, how, when, where) related to physical, physiological, psychological and occupational aspects which are just stimuli for causing stress and distress. Psychological and occupational stressors have taken the centre stage in today's world. Stress in the present age is ever increasing. A stressor may simply be defined as an event or situation, which induces stress. The following explains various aspects of stressors:-

1. **Physical:** It includes extreme temperature and humidity, noise, vibration, lack of oxygen and situations arising due to natural calamities such as famine, floods, earthquakes, tides and cyclones etc.

2. **Physiological:** It includes fatigue, poor physical condition, hunger, pain, strain, acute and chronic diseases.

3. **Psychological:** It relates to emotional factors which burden one's mind while coping up with the situations arising from many situation and circumstances such as:

    - A death or illness in the family,
    - Poor interpersonal relationship with family and relatives,
    - Loss of confidence, inferiority complex, emotional disturbances (anger, jealousy, hatred), Low Intelligence Quotient, Emotional Quotient, and Spiritual Quotient,

indecisiveness, dilemma etc,
- Wrong habits, addiction, laziness, carelessness, inability to manage time properly, fear, apprehensions, expectations, comparisons, competitions, exclamations etc,
- Various mental drives or urges such as: sensual pleasures, self love, self praise, lust for power, property, authority etc,
- Justice delayed or denied,
- No job opportunity, corruption etc.

4 **Occupational:** It relates to the factors inducing stress at work places, such as–
- Business worries or financial worries,
- Lack of skills,
- Excessive work load, non cooperation from colleagues, indisciplined and inefficient subordinates and conflicting expectations of superiors,
- Poor interpersonal relationship with colleague or boss,
- Inability to adjust with frequent changing policy of government and employer,
- Non-redressal of grievances,
- Lack of involvement in decision-making and unhealthy environment,
- Personality factors etc.

So stress has nothing to do with the outside, it has everything to do with the inside. Outside forces are just stimuli on which one reacts or pro-acts from inside according to the right or wrong perception of the mind. Seeking causes for it outside is just looking for a scapegoat. We use our manipulative minds to project that the causes for tension are outside stimuli.

When you enter a dark room you may collide with a chair and get hurt. Showering your anger on the chair, in such a situation, is meaningless. **Darkness is the problem. Tension comes from darkness – the inner darkness of ignorance.** Darkness inside exists in our thought processes that make us grope constantly in the darkness and creates tension in mind. Thus, the most important factor of stress is our mis-programmed mind due to ignorance. That is why, anger has occupied the place of intellect, self-consciousness has been replaced by selfish consciousness, courage has been replaced by fear and diseases have replaced health. Reflect on the following story–

Walking through a forest, a man chanced to meet four beautiful women. Greeting them, he introduced himself. The tall and slim woman said, "My name is *Buddhi* (Intellect), I live in man's head." The woman with kohl lined eyes said, "I am *Lajja*, and I live in the eyes of man as modesty and present myself as decorum in behaviour." The third lady had a well-toned body, "I live in man's heart. I give him the courage to live." The traveller bowed low. The fourth lady had rosy cheeks and radiated freshness. "My name is *Tandurusti* (Health). I live in man's stomach," she said.

As the traveller went ahead, his thoughts went back to the four women he had met. At the end of the forest, he met four young men. "I am *Krodh* (Anger)" said the first man who was handsome but for his brows, which were always knitted. "Where do you live?" the traveller asked. "I live in man's head", said *Krodh*. The traveller said this was not possible. He had just met Buddhi and she lived in the head. *Krodh* said, "Till I enter, *Buddhi* remains. Once I enter, she runs away." *Krodh* had strong muscles and a forceful personality. The second man was *Laalach* (Greed). "I live in people's eyes," he said. Once again the traveller interjected to say, "Only *Lajja* lives there". The greed answered, "Just place a bag of gold coins and see how *Lajja* runs away from people's eyes. Or offer a position of power. Desire does not believe in modesty, shame or decorum."

Who was the third man? "I am *Bhay* (Fear), the sickly-looking man said, "I live in people's heart." "Is it not the residence of *Himmat*?" The traveller asked. "When people do not obey their conscience, they are always afraid. They do wrong and so are full of fear of being caught. That is why *Himmat* wanders homeless while I reside comfortably in people's hearts. Sometimes when I dominate, people say they have a heart attack and go to the doctor. And thereby they give me even more space."

"My name is *Rog* (Disease)", said the fourth man. He looked healthy. "I live in people's stomach. They are forever downing intoxicants that go into their stomach, feeding me. I know you will wonder where *Tandurusti* goes. She does not stand a chance. Everybody wants her but it is me they feed when they drink, smoke and partake of other such substances."

●●●

10

EFFECTS OF STRESS

Effects of Stress

Stress has harmful effects not only on person's state of mind and his body but also on his family, social and professional life. The pressure and resulting stress may have adverse results, such as job dissatisfaction, reduced work effectiveness, behaviour changes or health damage. There are various conditions related to stress. Some of the important ones are alcoholism, headaches, heart diseases, stroke, hypertension, ulcers, psychosis and neurosis. On the whole, it affects the holistic health of the stressed person in the following ways:

Effects of Stress on Body
(Physical Symptoms)

1. **Affects physical health :** Mental stress is a trigger for angina as physical stress. Incidents of acute stress have been associated with a higher risk of serious cardiac events, such as heart rhythm abnormalities and heart attacks and even death from such events in people with heart disease.

   Some health effects caused by stress are reversible and the body and mind reverts to normal when the stress is relieved, but other health effects caused by stress are so serious that they are irreversible and at worse are terminal.

2. **Causes psychosomatic pains :** Too much stress can cause relatively minor illness like backaches, headaches, chronic fatigue, ulcer, etc.

3. **Causes life threatening diseases :** Stress can contribute

to potentially life threatening diseases like high blood pressure and heart diseases. Stress is also a leading contributor to death. *There is a direct relationship between heart disease, stroke, cancer and stress.*

Disabilities like hypertension, coronary artery disease (CAD), diabetes and psychiatric ailments are by and large multifactorial in nature and also have some element of stress involved. Many studies have confirmed the association between stress and hypertension. In recent years, increasing attention has been devoted to the interaction between stress, behavioural patterns and atherogenesis (formation of deposits on the innermost layer of arterial walls). Several important observations suggest that neuropsychological aberrations play an important role in the development and clinical expression of human atherosclerosis (a form of arteriosclerosis characterised by the deposition of atheromatous plaques containing cholesterol and lipids on the innermost layer of the walls of large and medium-sized arteries).

Apparently it seems that various **cancers** are caused due to the fast multiplication of the cells. In fact, there are other factors which induce the fast multiplication of the cells. Among these factors psychological stress is an important one. Hormonal and metabolic disturbances, which are observed during stress, lead to derailment of compensation and the derailment of adaptation. Such disturbances increase the multiplication of the cells in a susceptible organ.

4. **Reduces immunity power :** Stress breaks down the immune system leaving space for opportunistic diseases. Chronic stress produces a 'fight or flight' state, which may lead to high levels of stress inducing hormones in the body. Thus it reduces the resistance power of the body to fight against infective organisms. During stress defence mechanisms of the body are reduced due to increased level of steroid hormones, epinephrine, norepinephrine, uric acid, free fatty acid and cholesterol.

Disturbances of collagen synthesis, suppression of immunological defence mechanism and increase in muscle tension are observed during psychological stress. These changes can cause or precipitate **rheumatoid arthritis** and a host of other illnesses. Every stressful event takes away some of the reserve capacity of the body. Only when the normal four to eight fold reserve of an organ is exhausted, one experiences the symptoms of the disease.

5. **Causes Sleep disorder :** Sleep gets disturbed during stress and one suffers from sleeplessness and restlessness. This further causes several diseases.

6. **Biochemistry of physical body changes :** Stress activates adrenal gland, which produces more adrenalines, and cortisol hormones. This raises BP and heart beats· and releases bad cholesterol known as LDL (Low Density Lipoproteins), which further blocks coronary arteries, which causes heart attack. Stress prohibits the secretion of digestive enzymes and juices, which further causes constipation, gastric, acidity and gastrointestinal problems. Stress also causes headache and increased flow of blood in hair like capillaries, which gets ruptured and causes brain tumor and cancer at later stages.

7. **Causes diabetes :** Chronic stress has been associated with the development of insulin-resistance which is a primary factor in diabetes. Stress can also exacerbate existing diabetes by impairing the patient's ability to manage the disease effectively. To minimize fluctuations in blood glucose, a patient should balance medication, meal plans and exercise along with stress. Stressful changes in the life circumstances and psycho-physiologic state of a person with diabetes may conceivably lead to changes in levels of circulating hormones and to deviations from normal blood glucose levels-even though insulin or oral hypoglycemic (lowering the concentration of glucose in the blood) agents, meal plan, and exercise are held relatively constant. Such hormones include cortisol, catecholamines, glucagon, growth hormon, and beta- endorphin.

Stress in diabetic cases causes paralysis. Stress is the root of all diseases.

Effects of Stress on Mind
(Mental and Emotional Symptoms)

1. **Reduces memory power:** Stress significantly reduces brain functions such as memory, intellectual efficiency and even brings premature old age. It affects our concentration and learning all of which are central to effective performance at work. Certain tests have shown up to fifty percent loss of performance in cognitive tests performed on stress sufferers.

2. **Causes anger, irritability and anxiety:** There is a profound feeling of unhappiness during stress. The person feels constantly agitated and irritated due to demands made by the stressor. There is frequent outburst of anger and rage. He easily gets into arguments and shows his dissatisfaction through aggression. When we experience stress, serotonin levels in the brain are reduced. Chronic stress can lead to anxiety, general irritability and crankiness. Chronic stress can exacerbate symptoms of already existing medical conditions. Following an exceptionally stressful event some people with no previous psychiatric history develop a characteristic pattern of systems that include a sense of bewilderment, anxiety, anger, depression, over activity and withdrawal. Depression is usually the consequence of long-term stress and symptoms often occur with anxiety. Depression can be a disabling condition and like anxiety disorders, may result from untreated chronic stress. Studies suggest that the inability to adapt to stress is associated with onset of depression or anxiety. Some evidence suggests that repeated release of stress hormone produces hyperactivity in the hypothalamus-pituitary-adrenal axis and disrupts normal levels of serotonin, the nerve chemical that is critical for feeling of 'well being'.

   As per latest experiments, intestines get filled with blood due to indignation during stress, which further weakens digestive system.

3. **Stress causes confusion, loss of concentration and judgment power:** Stress causes confusion. Stress affects

concentration and judgement power, which further reduces the performance of people of every profession and **causes accidents**. So it is very important to deal with stress right at the beginning.

4. **Causes mental pollution:** Stress creates negative and wasteful thoughts in our mind to pollute us mentally. Mental pollution due to stress and distress radiates negative vibrations in surroundings. Nature too gets affected when our own nature gets polluted. There is deep interconnection between our own nature and nature outside. One of the examples of this is the growing ecological imbalances in nature due to mass deforestation and killing of wild animals.

5. **Creates a sense of insecurity, fear and frustration:** Stress creates a sense of insecurity. Insecurity may be related to one's life, lives of family members, finances, society, profession etc. These insecurities further create fears (False Evidences Appearing Real for Self). These fears keep agitating the mind and create frustration and distress in one's life. Life become insecure and gets trapped in the vicious circle of stress and distress.

Effects of Stress on Behaviour
(Behavioural Symptoms)

1. **Causes eating disorder and leads to obesity:** It leads to either excessive eating or drastic reduction in appetite. Stress can have varying effects on eating problems and weight. Often stress is related to weight gain and obesity. Many people develop cravings for salt, fat, and sugar to counteract tension and thus gain weight. This weight gain is often abdominal fat, a predictor of diabetes mellitus and heart ailments.

   Obesity is also frequently associated with hyperlipidemia (an excess of fats or lipids in the blood, also called hyperlipemia) and low HDL *[(high density lipoprotein)- a complex of lipids and proteins in approximately equal amounts that functions as a transporter of cholesterol in the blood.*

Science of Mind Simplified

High levels are associated with a decreased risk of atherosclerosis and coronary heart disease]. Thus, most of the evidence would suggest that obesity by itself is not a major risk factor but is an important underlying factor in a large proportion of diabetics in relation to other risk factors e.g. hypertension and dyslipidemia (a condition marked by abnormal concentrations of lipids and lipoproteins in the blood). The association of obesity with hypertension seems to be more significant and this could be an important factor in those studies where obesity and hypertension may not have been analyzed separately. The reversible nature of mild hypertension with weight loss has been re-emphasized in other large-scale studies.

2. **Causes behavioural changes:** The person withdraws from social life, avoids gatherings and becomes a loner. Family life further moves from bad to worse and worse to worst. Good relations suffer due to irritation and anger.

3. **Causes professional incompetency and low job satisfaction:** Stress causes physical, emotional and behavioural disorders, loss of memory and lack of concentration, which affects professional competency. A professional incompetency further leads to low productivity and job dissatisfaction.

4. **Get trapped in the vicious circles of negativity:** A stressed person gets trapped in the vicious cycle of negative actions and reactions. Spiritual powers get blocked. Individual becomes atheist. Stress further causes spiritual disharmony and religious intolerance. Demon of communalism gets stronger. Epidemic of psychological stress and distress spreads everywhere and creates negativity in environment.

5. **Leads to addiction and bad habits:** People under chronic stress frequently seek relief through drug or alcohol abuse, tobacco use, abnormal eating patterns or passive activities, such as watching television. The physiological effects of stress compound the damage. These self- destructive habits

become a vicious cycle. And the cycle is self-perpetuating. A sedentary routine, an unhealthy diet, alcohol abuse and smoking, promotes heart disease and interferes with sleep patterns. This would in turn lead to increased rather than reduced tension levels.

Thus, we have seen how stress and distress have cascading effects on not only individual but on society, nation and nature also.

•••

11

'A' TO 'Z' STEPS OF STRESS MANAGEMENT

Stress is like a comma, not a full stop. It is like waves in the ocean. Ocean cannot be without waves. We must know surfing to enjoy waves in the ocean. To a skilled surfer, sea waves can be exhilarating but if the surfer is inexperienced, it could lead to disaster. Similarly, human life is like an ocean and stresses are its waves. Human life cannot be without stress. Therefore, we must know how to relax and manage stress.

Modern stress management teaches do's and don'ts to avoid stress. But how to nurture it, is not taught. Conventional psychologists have suggested a number of stopgap measures to reduce stress. But none of them gets to the root causes of stress. They merely seek to ameliorate currently stressful circumstances. Some of the ideas have been to change the job, to find more leisure time, to find someone to talk about one's thought, to take up a hobby or to change one's lifestyle. The more perceptive doctors counsel the making of deeper psychological changes that are; to be honest with oneself and others, to act with maturity and to make decisions firmly to give up artificial crutches like alcohol and drugs to increase one's personal strength.

All of these goals may be good, yet the question remains how does one get the inner strength ever to make those changes? How does one get peace and clarity of mind to realise what steps are really necessary and possible to affect those changes and how does one get the flexibility to live even in what may be considered "stressful" circumstances since it is not always possible to change external conditions without feeling distressed by them?

To manage stress, we must know about self, aim and object of human life and the solutions of problems faced by human beings during their lives. There is A to Z practical steps (in subsequent chapters), which enable and empower the self to make changes in the lifestyle to lead a stress free and peaceful life and enjoy adventures of life like wind surfing.

A– "AWARENESS OF SELF AND AURA"

Ten students were crossing a river. After they crossed, they wanted to carry out a check to ensure that everyone had safely crossed the river. All of them came and stood in a single line. One of them came out and started counting. He could find only nine people. All of them got upset, because there was one person missing.

Another person came out of the line and started counting. He too could find only nine people. They could not find the tenth person. They confirmed that the tenth person might have got drowned.

At that time, a saint was passing by the side of the river. He heard their problem and counted the people in the line. He then turned his finger towards the person who was counting and arrived at a total of ten. He said that the tenth person was none other than the person who was counting the rest of them.

Similarly, we never count ourselves and think that we are the body only. We never differentiate ourselves from the body and even introduce ourselves with name, age, colour, sex, caste, occupation etc. of our physical body. One has to find and know the self to know the real mystery of life.

Awareness of Self and Aura: Awareness means understanding of inner as well as outer system of self and body. Physical body is the resultant of our inner body.

That is why, a healthy life means 'heal thy life' (inner body healing which means presence of all primary virtues or basic qualities for a life).

Kirlan Camera can take photograph of inner body.

Presence of all primary virtue creates a perfect aura, which serves as a shield to the physical body. There is a continuous radiation of colours and vibration of our inner body through our thoughts, emotions and visualisation. Non-radiation of any colour of virtues creates a hole in the aura, which is shielding our physical body from the bad effects of planets and stars. People use gems of different colours as a substitute of particular colours and vibration.

But this is a temporary shield and its effect depends upon its reality in lifestyle. Waste and negative thoughts destroy the aura. Therefore, planets and stars easily affect our physical and mental state. Thus, we are ourselves responsible for our own course of action, direction and condition. This is the truth, which we need to be aware of.

Awareness of truth enlightens us and the darkness of ignorance gets vanished. This is what we pray to God *"Tamso Ma Jyotirgamaya, Asado Ma Sadgamaya and Mrityo Ma Amritam Gamaya"*. When we move from darkness of ignorance to the light of knowledge, from untruth to truth and from mortality of physical body to immortality of our own inner subtle body, we get illuminated and become the perennial fountain of Knowledge, Peace, Purity, Love, Happiness, Bliss and Powers.

Application of "Tilak" on forehead means awareness of self as a source of pure energy positioned at Agya chakra. It is internal and not external to show others.

Tying the "Thread" in the right hand means tying mental body with right consciousness of primary virtues. This is also internal. External thread tied in right hand will neither purify mental energy nor protect physical body.

Ignorance of Self has Altered Our Perception of Primary Virtues or core values: Ignorance has replaced our primary virtues with wrong understanding and perception. It is evident by the following table:

Sl. No.	Primary core values virtues	Impressions in Standard File, which is inactive	Replaced Impressions in Waste Files, which is active
1.	Knowledge	Knowledge of Self, Supreme & Universal Eternal Cycle	Information of many field known as General Knowledge or identifying self as body.
2.	Purity	Purity of Thoughts, Speech and Action	External Cleanliness or External Beauty
3.	Peace	Peace of Mind and absence of waste and negative thoughts.	Absence of Sound, Calm and Cool, Pin drop Silence in Environment
4.	Love	Love for God and for all Human Beings	Lust, Opposite Sex Attraction
5.	Happiness	Contentment is the root of all happiness.	Conditional happiness, Comfortable Lifestyle with Modern Gadgets
6.	Power	Will Power and Eight Spiritual Powers	Money Powers, Positions, Status and Muscle Powers
7.	Bliss	Deep silence in true self consciousness. It is a joy beyond sense organs.	Enjoying with sensual pleasures, involving sense organs for drawing pleasures.

Self Awareness for Virtuous Lifestyle: In order to be virtuous continually we must maintain soul-consciousness – the awareness that we are eternal soul with the original attributes of Truth, Peace, Love, Joy, Purity, Power and Bliss. If we are able to maintain this awareness, virtues will have their field day. In other words, the chain of Awareness – Thought – Decision – Action – Result becomes positive. Intellect is the faculty that can ensure this positive chain but the strength required to determine which thoughts arise in the mind will be available to the intellect only when we are soul-conscious. When we are not soul-conscious, we are naturally body-conscious and in this state of consciousness the chain of awareness, thought-decision – action-result becomes negative. At any moment, positive and negative thoughts arising from experiences recorded as impressions (*sanskars*) vie with each other for space on the screen of mind. Thoughts coloured by emotions alternate between fear and determination as propelled by the memories *(sanskars)*. The intellect fights to choose between the oscillating flow of thoughts. Finally, when the intellect decides to act positively drawing on impressions (*sanskars*) of courage, the victory experienced.

B – BELIEVE YOURSELF (BELIEF SYSTEM)

We have two kinds of belief systems – 'macro' and 'micro' based on which the intellect functions.

Macro belief system involves large values like moral or ethical, governmental, religious and philosophical codes. These are the tenets that define us as Hindu, Muslim, Christian, Sikh and so on. Other beliefs related to a particular doctrine, organization, country or attitudes like feminism, intellectualism etc. also come under the macro belief system.

Micro belief system involves personal experiences and family beliefs. From an early age, you choose the behaviours that give you love and safety in your family. You incorporate the values acceptable in your family and the world around into your belief system. These are often, both subtle and unconscious.

Belief systems get cemented, first by family attitudes, later by religions, school, television shows, friends and so on. If you hold an image of yourself as worthless, every single decision you make will reflect that belief system and you create conditions that make your life worthless. Abusive relationships reinforce your bad self-image.

Universal law of belief: The Universal law of belief says that whatever we believe with feeling, becomes our reality. We don't believe what we see; instead, we see what we

believe. Our beliefs form a screen as to how we see the world and we never allow any information that is not consistent with our beliefs to pass through it. Even if we have beliefs that are totally inconsistent with reality, we won't let them through because our beliefs have become true for us.

Wrong belief or most harmful belief: The most important quality you can ever develop is having belief in yourself. The beliefs that you form without a shadow of a doubt achieve success in every area of your life. Virtually every person has the capacity to do wonderful things with his or her life, but the greatest single obstacle for most people is self-doubt. Many people wish they could accomplish certain things but lack the belief that they can actually do it.

You form your self-image based on how people see you, what you believe about yourself, and your attitude towards others and the world. This self image affects everything you do, feel, desire or fear and it affects your vibrations too. Your family, employers and acquaintance perpetuate or enhance your feeling of worthlessness.

When people said to achieve in any part of their life, it is their beliefs more than anything else that holds them back. Self-limiting beliefs act as breaks on our ability to achieve our goals. Many of us have high hopes, dreams, and aspirations, but we let doubts creep in to our mind and undermine our talents, abilities and effectiveness.

Each one of us has feelings of inferiority because we feel that we are not good enough. We think that we are not as good as other people are and we feel that we are not good enough to acquire and enjoy the things we want in life. Often we feel that we don't deserve good things. Even if we work hard and have some achievements in our life, we often feel that we are not really entitled to our successes.

The most common and the most harmful beliefs are the ones that are self-limiting. These are beliefs about yourself. For example, believing that you can't achieve something because you don't have enough money or education. You might believe you can't achieve something because you are from the wrong sex, race, age, or it is because of the economy. Most of these beliefs are not true, but they will hold you back nonetheless.

How to change your belief?

The fact is, you deserve every good thing that you are capable of acquiring through the use of your talents. The only real limitation you can have is your lack of desire. If you set a goal and want to achieve it badly enough, nothing in the world can stop you from achieving it, as long as you are willing to persist long and hard enough. Do the following to change your beliefs: -

1. Set your goal: To develop positive beliefs, you have to decide exactly where you want to end up in the future. The clearer you are about the result you want in your future, the easier it will be for you to change your actions and behaviour in the short term. This in turn, will assure that you achieve what you want in the long term.

Once you have clearly decided on the type of person you want to be, you will have already taken a major first step in developing new beliefs.

Ponder over the following –

A young man came to meet Buddha. But he was not aware that he was the enlightened Buddha. He was so enamoured by the brightness and beauty of his presence that he asked him...

"Are you a Celestial being?"

"No", he replied.

"Have you descended from the heavens?", he asked.

"No", replied Buddha.

"Then are you from this earth?", he questioned.

"No", came the answer.

Now the young man lost his patience and said, "then, who are you?"

"Oh, son, you could have asked this question at the very outset," said Buddha. "I am a clean mirror, just reflecting what is."

Please note that what is reflected does not pollute the mirror. If our consciousness can be like a mirror, then our life will have a different flavour.

This is a famous saying of Buddha. It has a very deep meaning.

When someone praises us as "Capable or Clever", what do we think?

We feel, "this person says I am intelligent, he thinks I know a lot, he calls me clever, he compares me with Chanakya, he feels that I am highly skillful and he is astounded at my intelligence. In this manner, we heap words of praise in exchange for a single word of appreciation.

Similarly, if someone calls us a fool, we add a thousand words of insult and feel depressed.

But if our mind were like a plain mirror as Buddha said, then we would reflect only on the word spoken by the other person. We would not look into every possible interpretation of the word, and create meanings, which do not exist. We will keep our focus very clear and will reflect on our goal through our actions.

2. In order to incorporate your new beliefs into your everyday life discipline yourself with that thought and situation: You have to discipline yourself to act exactly in every situation as if you already were that person. When you begin to act like the successful person you want to become, you will actually adopt his values, qualities, and characteristics, and they will then become a permanent part of your personality. Never have any undercurrent of negative faith or just depend on God without doing anything. God helps those who help themselves.

Reflect on the following story: A lady was sitting by the side of a window watching the scene outside. The mountain was very pretty. Suddenly she remembered a proverb "Prayers can move mountains". She wanted to test God.

Closing her eyes, she knelt on the floor and prayed thus: "God, if you move this mountain that is between the sea and my house, I will get the sea breeze, so please move the mountain."

When she opened her eyes, the mountain was intact, without having moved an inch. She smiled and said, "I was very sure that the mountain would not move. The saying that prayers can move mountain is all baloney. My hunch that it would not, was correct," and patted herself.

She prayed with a conviction that her prayer would not move the mountain. The essence of the prayer came from disbelief rather than belief. Here, prayer was a mere ritual and not an expression of commitment.

3. **Consistently visualise your mission and vision:** If you consistently act like the person you want to become everyday and in every situation it will begin a chain reaction. Your attitude will change and become more positive. This will then build stronger and more positive beliefs. And your beliefs will exert a positive influence on your values.

You have no limitations on your potential except for those that you believe you have. Successful people are not extraordinary or special in any way. They are not different from you or me. But, all successful people do have the unwavering belief that they can accomplish anything that they really want in life. You are a good person. From today onwards, see yourself as the very best you can be, and refuse to accept any limitations on your possibilities. **Once you develop that belief in yourself, and you act in accordance with your beliefs, your future will be unlimited. Your vision of success has to be realised.**

Reflect on following vision of success: There was a multi-national company making shoes. In order to assess the level of demand for their shoes, the director of the company deputed a manager to a country in Africa. The manager cut short his tour with a report "We cannot sell any shoes in that country". When asked for an explanation, he said, "People walk bare foot; no one wears shoes there. Hence no potential."

The director was not a man to accept "No" for an answer. So he sent another man to study the situation. On his return, jumping with joy, he declared, "There is a huge market for our shoes in that country."

"How is that?", asked the Director.

"People walk bare foot; no one wears shoes in the whole country. Hence, huge potential for our product, was the reply.

This is what we have to learn from the above story. Every person's experience is different in situations like work, trade, home.... but as far as I can see, all experiences can be categorised into two types – good and bad. Whatever the experience, if a lesson can be learnt from, it is a good one. If one cannot learn or has not learnt a lesson from it, it is a bad one.

In every situation see a possibility and have a vision of success; like the manager saw the possibility of selling shoes in a place where people were not wearing shoes. His vision of success multiplied the company's growth and profits.

4. Never limit yourself with wrong beliefs: If someone calls us "lazy" we get affected by that word only when we take it to be ours. If we are clearly and firmly aware that we are not lazy, what that person says about us is just nonsense. "Nonsense" would never affect us. In fact, we would not pay any heed to a person who speaks nonsense.

If someone calls me lazy and I am deeply affected, it only reflects on my true nature of being lazy. Others point out the quality in me. This is the root cause for getting affected. This gives rise to blood pressure and tension.

Without labeling your thoughts as good or bad add without showing any aversion to your thoughts, take an impartial stand and notice your thoughts. This is known as seeing things through a bird's eyes.

Whether the thoughts are sad, tempting or happy, without identifying them with yourself, when you view them from a distance a clear understanding will crystallize within you.

Once this mental state is attained, sadness and happiness will appear as two sides of the same coin. Happiness is an experience. Similarly sadness is also another experience. For people who do not have peace of mind and clarity, even happiness will appear as an experience of sadness.

Reflect on the following story: Once Buddha went to beg with his disciple Ananda. When they approached a house for food, the lady of the house spoke harshly. "You lazy fellows, you are hale and hearty...why can't you work for your food?" She yelled and chased them away. The disciple was enraged at the woman for using such hostile words for his great *Guru*.

"Please permit me to teach that woman a solid lesson" he pleaded with Buddha. But Buddha walked away in silence.

A little later, Buddha handed over his water container to Ananda and went to take rest.

Having rested for a couple of hours they resumed their journey. On the way, Buddha glanced at the water container and asked, "whose is this?" "It is yours, *Guruji*", said Ananda. Buddha took it and looked at it once and returned it to Ananda saying; "No I gifted it to you a little while ago...it is yours."

At night, Buddha pointed to the same water container and asked once again, "Whose is this?" Now Ananda said, "*Guruji* it is mine."

Hearing this, Buddha said laughingly, "I asked you the same question earlier this evening and you said it was mine. Now you are saying, it is your. How can the same container be yours and mine at the same time?"

Though Ananda was slightly confused, he replied calmly, "*Guruji*, you said that you have gifted this container to me and I accepted it. Hence, I said that it was mine. Initially, when you gave it to me I did not consider it as mine, because even though you had handed over the container to me, it was still yours."

Buddha smiled at Ananda and said, "Similarly, I did not take the words the lady spoke harshly as mine; I did not accept them. So, even though the words were spoken to me, they still belonged to the lady alone. That is the reason I said that there was no need to teach her a lesson. This advice from Buddha to his disciple expounds a very simple truth.

Don't Label Yourself With What Others Say–Think in A Positive Way

5. Develop creativity and a sense of humour to make your beliefs firm: To be creative is a basic need in everyone. Hence, allow this force to emerge and make yourself firm. At least, start being creative by cracking jokes and calm your mind to remain creative.

When you crack a joke, more than the joke, the laughter that remains in your being is nourishing. Laughter creates a deep silence and in that silence, the problematic and serious mind dissolves. Jokes work very interestingly. You are saying something and there is an unexpected twist in your presentation, and that creates a new surprise, a new joy. The art of cracking a joke is a creative art.

Reflect on the following example: A seven-foot tall man was about to get married. His married friends gave him a piece of advice. They said, "Right from the first day of marriage be strict with your wife or else she will be your master." Following the advice of his friends, on the very first night he commanded his wife, "Do you know who I am? I am a wrestler and my father was also a wrestler. Tomorrow, I expect hot water for my bath at 3 a.m. or else…"

The wife was scared. She got up at 2:30 a.m. and heated water for her husband.

This went on every day for months. Before retiring to bed he repeated, "Hot water for bath . _ .at 3 a.m. or else…."

The wife finally got fed up and one night when he repeated the same phrase she said," Okay. Or else what will you do?"

"Or else…. I will take a cold water bath", said the husband.

When one develops a humorous attitude to life, one's childlike nature emerges. There is a child in us, which wants to be free. As we grow older the child in us is suppressed and hence our playfulness also gets suppressed. Creativity and joy disappear when we have a serious attitude towards life.

Reflect on the following story of Rapunzel: Rapunzel was a great beauty. When she was young, a witch took her away from her parents and imprisoned her inside a tall tower, deep in a dense forest. The tower did not have doors or stairs. Right on top, there was just one single window. Rapunzel eventually grew into a beauty, with skin like fresh blown roses and long hair like spun gold.

Rapunzel grew up knowing nothing about the outside world. The witch used to visit her through a window, climbing by grasping her long hair. But the witch did not reveal to her as to how beautiful she was. She was very possessive of her and did not ever want her to leave the tower. She thought, if Rapunzel learnt of her true nature, or of the world outside she would escape from her and go away. There was nothing in the tower that could reflect anything; so the girl had never even seen her own face. All she knew was the witch.

The witch constantly told Rapunzel how ugly she was and demeaned her totally, from dawn to dusk. Rapunzel had no choice but to believe all this. She used to feel sad that God had created her ugly and cried bitterly, all day long.

Once a prince saw her and got attracted towards her beauty. He told Rapunzel that she was the most beautiful girl he had ever seen. Later he got her out from the clutches of wicked witch and married her.

Wrong Belief is Like A Witch, Creativity is the Prince

Similarly, there is a witch of negative belief, which has kept us at the tower of isolation by repeated thoughts of frustration and depression. The prince is the creativity, which saw the beauty of standard file of our memory and motivated us to get rid of the negative and blind belief.

There was a young boy who was repeatedly told by his parents and others that he was very weak in English language and could not learn English. This young boy, just like Rapunzel believed what others said about him as the whole truth and nothing but the truth. He even avoided reading English newspapers and magazines. He refused to speak even a few words in English, to others. If at all, he faced a situation where he was forced to speak English, he would slip away, excusing himself saying, "I cannot speak English."

This way of frequently telling oneself is known as Repetitive Thinking. The tall tower represents repetitive thinking.

It is like an ox bound to a wooden log in an oil-mill, moving on the same track again and again. Just as Rapunzel was imprisoned in a tall tower, this young man was imprisoned by his own repetitive thinking. Due to this thinking, he never even attempted to learn English.

To develop this boy's self confidence, a prince must come along. That prince is what I call "Creativity". Only this prince can overcome the witch that is "Negative Belief". The prince – "Creativity" alone can release the princess – Ability from the prison of Repetitive Thinking.

Feeling shy of speaking English is only one such example. Life is replete with many examples. When we are faced with people such as a prejudiced boss, a debtor who refuses to repay the loan, a spouse who is always rude... if we think with a repetitive mind that one can never change such characters, we cannot find any solution to our problems. *In order to plan how to approach them, think clearly; the most essential tool for all of us is "Creativity".*

NO ONE CAN MAKE YOU FEEL INFERIOR
WITHOUT YOUR CONSENT
(Eleanor Roosevelt)

C – COUNSELLING FOR JOB RELATED STRESS

Stress related to incompetence, low motivation, over pressure, unreasonable performance demands, office politics, lack of recognition, change of duty etc. are to be dealt with very effectively. In such cases, a detailed analysis should be done and the following therapy should be provided:

- Previous records should be checked to compare his performance. Inputs from boss and colleagues should be gathered. It is very important to check if there is some other problem related to family or health that is interfering with his work.
- Convince employees that their contributions are significant and their shortcomings should be carefully handled.
- Rotate employees out of potentially stressful positions and do not allow them to overwork.
- Organize training programmes to help employees cope with stress.
- Exhaustive counselling session should be provided.
- Emergency actions should be over learnt to the point of automation and frequently rehearsed.

Flying has many stresses inherent in it. Intelligent appreciation of the situation, split second decisions and skilled actions are required to meet them successfully. Human capacity for these activities tends to suffer under stress and emotionally upsetting. There are large individual differences in emotional stability and stress resistance. Stress cannot be avoided but it can be managed so that it doesn't hamper growth. Effective stress management can be achieved by counselling. Many a time, a professional advice is essential to make the best decision.

Counselling can help to raise motivational levels, boost morale, and improve interpersonal relationship, performance and good health. Stress if not managed timely can be very harmful for the integrity of the person as a whole.

D – DISCIPLINE YOUR MIND

Discipline means inner discipline of our mind, intellect and memory. Today our mind has enslaved the being, intellect has been corrupted to give wrong judgements and memory is active with waste and negative files and the self has become powerless to assert itself

Without inner discipline, our life cannot be reconciled with external disciplined way of life. Discipline plays a vital role in getting 100% marks (4+9+19+3+9+16+12+9+15+5=100, where A=1, D=4 and so on) for success in life.

The state of the self and the state of the environment are intimately interconnected through **Mind - body relationships and society**. A healthy and disciplined state of each one of these factors will make the world a better place to live. The original, healthy and disciplined states of all the six factors (Self, Mind, Body, Relationships, Society, and Environment) are given below;

The original states of the self are: bliss (balance), truth (knowledge), peace, love, joy, purity, power and so on.

The original states of the mind are: positivity, harmony, balance, discipline etc.

The original states of the body are: health, vitality, balance etc.

The original states of the relationships are: harmony, respect, sincerity etc.

The original states of the society are: order, cooperation, justice, tolerance etc.

The original states of the environment are: cleanliness, harmony, balance etc.

The states of all these six factors are interdependent. The states of the environment or society encompass all other states. The seed of both the problems and the solutions is the state of the self. To change the self is to change the world. The awareness- thought- decision- action- result are cyclically repeat based on the law of cause and effect. Body consciousness creates a negative chain and soul consciousness creates a positive chain.

When there is a desire for pure experience and the realization of the importance of the quality of thought, then the intellect selects those seeds (thoughts) that will bear the desired fruit. If I desire peace, contentment, love, joy, and power I will try to eradicate those thoughts and *sanskars*, which are the seeds of disharmony and peacelessness. Positive and negative experiences recorded as *sanskars* often battle with each other for space on the screen of the mind. **My original disciplined state is the highest state of my consciousness.** To get back to that highest state again, I use the tools of my mind – thoughts and emotions. I perceive the height of my goal through the intellect. *I move towards the goal using the know-how in sanskars, disciplining of mind (thoughts and emotions, etc); using determination or will power of the intellect and keeping doubts at bay.*

Will power is my ability to put into practice the ideals I know to be for my well-being and to resist harmful activities. **In a weak and indisciplined soul**, intellect plays no role in determining which thoughts arise in the mind; they come as if driven by the *sanskars* (in the form of habits) or are triggered by the atmosphere or by the moods of others and create disharmony among these six factors.

How a disciplined Mind nurtures the nature outside: A village was starved of rain for many seasons. The fields were parched and the wells had dried. At that stage, a monk came to the village. People described their pathetic condition with tears in their eyes. The monk decided to relieve them of their sufferings. He requested for a place in the center of the village to meditate. During the course of his meditation, the rain God was pleased and showered the village with heavy rain. The villagers got drenched in joy. They gathered around the monk with tears of gratitude and exclaimed, "How did you manage to do this?"

The monk replied, "As I meditated, a sense of peace dawned on my mind and harmony set in my body. The atmosphere around me was in tune with harmony. The harmony created a difference externally thereby enabling transformation of the season of no rain. So it rained. If you are in harmony, nature will be in harmony with you."

If there were peace of mind within disciplined thoughts and emotions, the same would spread outwardly also. So is it with nature. If one does not cheat others, nature will not betray mankind. This was the philosophy proved by the zen monk.

A disciplined mind dances and makes our body dance in any situation. People dance because they are happy or occasion is a happy one but a disciplined mind dances to be happy at any moment of life.

E – EDGE OUT YOUR EGO

A woodpecker was pecking an oak tree. A lightening struck the tree and felled it. The woodpecker flew away and boasted, "I never knew I was so strong; I could make a tree fall."

Drop your ego. You will find people as God's messengers conveying divine messages to you, teaching you through their mistakes and successes.

Most of us are like an oak tree in a flowerpot. The flowerpot is like the ego and our being is like the oak tree. Do not limit yourself to the ego. Drop your lower self and let your higher self guide you. This is the meaning of yoga: being yoked to the higher self.

EGO means Edging God Out. When we fly into the sky of self-pride and ego, criticism chases us to make us exhausted and tired. When we are free of ego we get the vast sky of knowledge and wisdom to enjoy the journey of inner space.

Freedom is the universal law of living in this world. It has to be followed in words and spirit to live a tension free life and let others be tension free.

Reflect on the following: A crow found a piece of meat. The moment it picked up the piece of meat, the other crows and eagles began chasing it. The crow soared higher and higher to safeguard the meat. The others chased it relentlessly. At one point, the crow dropped the meat; the other crows and eagles that were chasing it, charged towards the meat that had fallen to the ground.

Now that the crow was free from the others, it realized a great truth.

"It is true that I have lost the meat, but then, I have obtained a great freedom."

The ego within us is very similar to this piece of meat. If you can drop it, then life will become buoyant. One need not have any tension. Just as the crow could enjoy the beauty of the vast sky, we too can see the beauty of life by dropping our ego.

Ponder over this story: There was an egoist king. Once when he went to the forest to hunt, he met a sage. The sage was meditating with his eyes closed. The king said, "I have won over many lands and have annexed them to my kingdom. My treasury overflows with riches that I have brought from various places. In my palace, there are many wonderful and pretty women from different regions, ready to please me. Yet I am not happy. When will I become happy?"

The sage, opening his eyes, screamed at him, "You will be happy only when I die," and closing them again, went back to meditation.

In a rage, the king drew out his sword to kill him, saying, "I am a great king. How dare you insult me thus?" The sage opened his eyes again and said, "Hey you fool. I did not mean myself when I said "I"... I meant the ego. When the ego dies, you will be happy."

If a person who has less education, status or wealth expresses an opinion contrary to our own, we do not accept it. It is our ego, which does not permit us to accept the same. We immediately react negatively.

There is an incident from the life of the famous personality R N Tagore. Once he was crossing the river Yamuna in a boat. It was night. Under candlelight Tagore tried to compose a poem. But somehow, the poetry would not flow. Finally, he gave up and put out the candle. The moment the candlelight went off, moonlight filled the boat and the boat appeared beautiful. Tagore experienced a great sense of beauty. At once, poetry began to flow out of his heart... effortlessly.

What is the connection here? The candlelight was capable of hiding the moonlight in the same way the petty ego hides the vast happiness of heart.

To Edge Out Ego, Go Within

A woodcutter was toiling to earn two meals a day. He met a monk. The monk advised him, "Drop being at the edge of the forest and go into the forest. Your daily hours of work will fetch you one-month's food."

The woodcutter followed the advice. Deep within the forest, he found sandalwood trees. He was very happy. He expressed his gratitude to the monk for having guided him.

The monk advised again, "Take the risk of going still deeper into the forest. A day's work will fetch you food for six months. Fortunately, this also turned out to be true; for he found a silver mine. He thanked the monk again, profusely. The monk further advised, "If you trust me and go further deep into the forest, a day's work will make you earn enough to fetch you food for a life time." This also turned out to be true; for he found a gold mine.

The woodcutter wondered, "Why then does the monk still stay at the edge of the forest and not venture into the forest, as he has been advising me?"

He expressed his doubts to the monk. The monk replied, "If you want to be eternally happy, sit under this tree and I will teach you to go within. Then you will be eternally happy."

To be an outer winner, one has to explore the outside world, to be an inner winner; one has to go within oneself. The kingdom of heaven is within us.

One should balance between being an outer and an inner winner. Only then would one feel good.

F – FORGIVE AND FORGET

God loves to express himself through us in harmony, peace, beauty, joy, love and prosperity. This is called the will of God or the tendency of life.

Many persons habitually set up mental resistance to the flow of life by accusing and reproaching God for the sin, sickness and suffering. Others cast the blame on God for their pains, aches, loss of loved ones, personal tragedies and accidents. They are angry with God, and they believe he is responsible for their misery.

As long as people, entertain such negative concepts about God, they will experience automatic negative reaction from their memory bank. What they fail to understand is that they are punishing themselves. They must see the truth, find release, and give up all condemnation, resentment and anger against anyone or any power outside themselves. Otherwise they cannot go forward into a healthy, happy or creative activity.

Remember Forgiveness is the Life Principle

The life-principle holds a bottomless fund of forgiveness for you. It forgives you when you cut your finger. The subconscious intelligence within you sets about immediately to repair it. New cells build bridges over the cut. If you burn your hand, the life principle reduces the edema and congestion and gives you new skin, tissue and cells.

Life holds no grudges against you. It is always forgiving you. Life brings you back to health, vitality, harmony and peace. If you co-operate by thinking in harmony with nature, negative, hurtful memories, bitterness and ill-will clutter up and impede the free flow of the life principle within you.

Forgiveness is a Necessary Condition for Healing

Forgiveness of others is essential for mental peace and radiant health. You must forgive everyone who has ever hurt you if you want perfect health and happiness. Forgive yourself by getting your thoughts in harmony with divine law and order. You cannot forgive yourself completely until you have forgiven others first. To refuse to forgive is nothing more or less than spiritual pride or ignorance.

In the psychosomatic field of medicine today, it is being constantly emphasised that resentment, condemnation of others, remorse and hostility are behind a host of maladies ranging from arthritis to cardiac disease. The stress caused by these negative emotions can directly affect the immune system of the body, leaving you open to infection and disease.

Specialists in stress related disorders point out that people who were hurt, maltreated, deceived or injured often react by filling themselves with resentment and hatred for those who hurt them. This reaction causes inflamed and festering wounds in their subconscious minds. There is only one remedy. They have to cut out and discard their hurts and the one and only sure way to do this is through forgiveness.

Art of Forgiveness

The essential ingredient in the art of forgiveness is the willingness to forgive. If you sincerely desire to forgive the others, you are more than halfway over the hurdle. Of course, you have to understand that to forgive another does not necessarily mean that you like him or want to associate with him or her. You cannot be compelled to like someone. However, we can love people without liking them. *Love means that you wish for the other – health, happiness, peace, joy and all the blessings of life.*

You are not being magnanimous when you forgive, you are really being selfish, because what you wish for the others, you are actually wishing for yourself. The reason is that you are thinking it and you are feeling it. As you think and feel, so are you.

Visualise the following (use your third eye) to bring about forgiveness in yourself. It will work wonders in your life as you practice it. Think of God and his love for you and visualize:

"I fully and freely forgive (think of the name and visualize the offender). I release him/her mentally and spiritually. I completely forgive everything connected with the matter in question. I am free and he/she is free. It is a marvellous feeling.

This is my day of general amnesty. I release anybody and everybody who has ever hurt me, and I wish for each and everyones' health, happiness, peace and all the blessings of life. I do this freely, joyously and lovingly. Whenever I think of the person or persons who hurt me, I say, "I have released you, and all the blessings of life are yours. I am free and you are free. It is wonderful."

The great secret of true forgiveness is that once you have forgiven the person, it is not necessary to repeat this prayer. Whenever the person comes to your mind or that particular pain happens to enter your mind, wish him and say, "May God give you peace and happiness." Do this as often as the thought enters into your mind. You will find that after a few days the thought of the person or experience will return less and less often, until it fades into nothingness.

Test Your Forgiveness

Prospectors and jewellers use what is called an acid test to tell if a metal is a real gold or an imitation. There is an acid test for forgiveness, too. Imagine that I tell you something wonderful about someone who has wronged you, cheated you, or defrauded you. If you sizzle at hearing the good news about this person, the root of hatred is still in your subconscious mind, playing havoc with you.

Suppose you had a very painful dental procedure last year and you tell me about it now. If I ask whether you are in pain from it now, you will give me an astonished look and say, "Of course not! I remember the pain, but I don't feel it any longer."

That is the whole story. If you have truly forgiven someone, you will remember the incident, but you will no longer feel the sting or hurt of it. This is the acid test of forgiveness. You must meet it psychologically and spiritually. Otherwise, you are simply deceiving yourself. You are not practicing the true art of forgiveness.

Appreciate the Forgiveness

If someone criticizes you and those faults are within you, rejoice, give thanks and appreciate the comments as this gives you the opportunity to correct the particular fault. Critics cannot hurt you when you know that you are the master of your thought, reactions and emotions. This gives you the opportunity to pray for and bless the other, thereby blessing yourself.

Forgiveness is the key that unlocks the door of resentment and the handcuffs of hate. It is a power that breaks the chains of bitterness and the shackles of selfishness. He who cannot forgive others destroys the bridge over which he himself must pass.

There was a man who saw a scorpion floundering around in the water. He decided to save it by stretching out his finger, but the scorpion stung him. The man still tried to get the scorpion out of the water, but the scorpion stung him again. Another man nearby told him to stop saving the scorpion that kept stinging him. But the man said, "It is the nature of the scorpion to sting. It is my nature to love. Why should I give up my nature to love just because it is the nature of the scorpion to sting?"

Don't give up loving. Don't give up your goodness even if the people around you sting.

While forgiving, bless him/her as follow:

May your thoughts be of flowers!

May your dreams be of love!

May the stars twinkling down on us be your ever-guiding love!

May you find hope in all your fear and fright!

May you find love that is only heard through the whispers of the night!

May we love one another and lose this fight!

May we all be equal in each other's sight!

May our tears be kissed away by hope and wisdom!

May you love yourself and others too!

May God give me courage to give love in all I do!

"MAN GETS AND FORGETS AND GOD GIVES AND FORGIVES. TO ERR IS HUMAN, TO FORGIVE IS DIVINE"

G – GET ON WITH GOD GIFTS

Remember past is a history, future is a mystery and present is the presents from god ("God Gift") to a human being to enjoy and utilize for shaping one's bright future. When you start facing problems and difficulties think that you are paying the dues of your past actions. Hence, feel happy about it and enjoy the gift of God. Gifts of God are all primary virtues and not physical wealth and health. Physical wealth and health are the by-products of primary virtues and our actions. God gives contentment, love, peace, powers etc. to apply in our action to get physical health and wealth. *God is the ocean of all virtues and not ocean of physical wealth etc. What is there in the ocean, we get that only.*

I ASKED GOD -

I asked God to take away my pain.

God said, "No,

It is not for me to take away, but for you to give it up."

I asked God to make my handicapped child whole.

God said, "No. Her spirit is whole and her body is only temporary."

I asked God to grant me patience.

God said, "No. Patience is a by-product of tribulations, it isn't granted, but it is earned."

I asked God to give me happiness.

God said, "No. I give you blessings. Happiness is up to you."

I asked God to spare me from suffering.

God said, "No. Suffering draws you apart from worldly cares and brings you closer to me."

I asked God to make my spirit grow.

God said, "No. You must grow on your own, but I will prune you to make you fruitful."

I asked for all things so that I might enjoy life.

God said, "No. I will give you life so that you may enjoy all things."

I asked God to help me love others, as much as he loves me.

God said...Ah, finally you have the idea. It is gifted to you.

It is unlimited PRABHU-PRASAD, give to all generously.

God Gifts

God has gifted us seven unique gifts known as **seven wonders of inner world.** We must go on an inner journey to enjoy these gifts.

Seven wonders of the inner world –

1. Treasures of knowledge and wisdom.
2. Palace of Peace
3. Temple of Purity
4. Fountain of Love
5. Highway of Happiness and Joy
6. Showers of Bliss
7. Powerful fort of Spiritual Kingdom.

Past is History, Brooding Over It Is To Destroy the God's Gifts

First, let us take a look at the past. The past is also known as the "dead past". But in the heart of our hearts, we do not allow the past to die. Even though we do not want it, we still carry it unnecessarily in our hearts and struggle with it.

There was a very proud village head. He would bow his head only in front of one person – that was the barber. One day, while having a hair cut, the barber asked, "Is it true that the owner of the neighbouring fields stopped water for your crops? Have the crops wilted?"

"Don't remind me of that," roared the man in a fierce rage.

"All right. Forget that. Have you had any news about your wife who ran away two years ago? Don't talk. Just shut up and mind your business," warned the village head.

Finally, when the haircut was over, the barber said, "Sir, please forgive me for being impertinent. When I talked about unpleasant events of your life, you got angry. Your hair arose and stood firm. It made my job easy. I wanted to give you a good haircut. That is why, I reminded you of your past. However, what I did was wrong; please forgive me."

So, if we recall misfortunes and difficulties that we faced in the past, our blood boils. Our heart becomes heavy and we feel dejected.

Future is Mystery, Apprehension of Future Snatches the Gifts of God

The anxiety and the fear of the future is the next stage. What will happen tomorrow? What will happen to the business? These very thoughts of uncertainty of future bring fear.

There is a way to live life without worrying about the past or being anxious of the future. If you ask someone, they will boastfully quote from the *Gita*: "Do your duty, do not expect results". Many do not understand the deeper meaning in this saying.

Result is related to the future. Duty is related to the present. If one worries about the future, the present work will be imbalanced. That is why it is said; "we must not worry about results".

While we tremble from the fear of the future, we must remember that the present is being wasted.

Just as we take the holy water in a temple in cupped hands, look at it with reverence, taste it lovingly and feel divine; we must enjoy the present moment with relish. If we are submerged in the fear of the future, we will miss many pleasant moments including seeing the beauty of our spouse and children. The tongue will lose the taste of delicious food. We will live our life like a mechanical robot.

Does this mean that one should not plan for the future? No. Please plan your future. Plan well. But do not worry constantly about it and thus live in fear. Plan for the future. Learn from the past. Enjoy the present.

The past might have been filled with sadness and the future may be uncertain. We do not know. Our present moment is the only gift given to us by God. To put it briefly –

Past is history,
Future is Mystery
Present is a Gift
That's why we call it PRESENT from God.

H – HARVEST HAPPINESS IN LIFE

Happiness is the harvest of quiet mind. Anchor your thoughts on peace, poise, security and divine guidance and your mind will be productive of happiness.

There is no block to your happiness. External things are not causative; they are effects, not causes. Take your cue from the only creative principle within you. Your thought is a cause and a new cause produces a new effect. Choose happiness.

The happiest person is the one who brings forth the highest and the best in him or herself. God is the highest and the best in him or her, for the kingdom of God is within.

When you give happiness to someone, happiness comes back to you with the same intensity. Hence, always give happiness to others and never even think of giving unhappiness to anyone. *But the seed of happiness is contentment.* People are always longing for lasting peace and happiness but they don't know how to harvest it.

Reflect on the following story: There is a story of a weaver who prayed devotedly to Lord Shiva to provide him with money to live comfortably. Every morning after prayers, he would walk around the Shiva temple a hundred times. But wealth never came to him. As time passed, walking around the temple became a physical strain for the weaver.

When Shiva did not responded to the weaver's prayer, Parvati asked him why he was so hard on the weaver. Shiva replied, "His destiny is not to be rich. If something is not in our destiny it will not happen." Still, Parvati implored Shiva to do something. "All right," Shiva said, "I will give him a pot of gold. Let us see what happens." So Shiva placed a pot of gold on the weaver's path and stood aside to watch.

The old weaver, while walking, prayed, "O Lord, I am grateful that my eyes are working and I can weave well." However, he suddenly became fearful. What will happen if I lose my eyesight in my old age, what if I am unable to walk around the temple? Let me see if I can walk with my eyes closed."

The weaver closed his eyes to check and thus he walked past the gold. When he opened his eyes, he was very happy and said to himself, "Even if I go blind I can come to the temple to worship."

Thus Shiva reiterated, the weaver was not destined to have wealth. Shiva however promised to help him. "The weaver has just realised that the things that make him happy are his work and worship. Instead of wealth, I will give him gratitude for what he has and that will make him contented and happy."

The weaver was praying for something not meant for him. Like him, we pray for things not in our karmic destiny. *Many people think that riches will bring them happiness, but real happiness is found when we learn to have contentment in life and when we turn towards a joy that is permanent.*

Contentment does not mean being complacent for further innovations and inventions and nurturing quality of life. Contentment should not be in quantity of life, which creates impediments in seeking truth but in creating harmony in relationship.

Happiness Does Not Lie in Renunciation

Someone told a rich man that there was happiness in a life of renunciation. So, he decided to try that too. He packed all his wealth, the treasure stored in his house, all diamonds, precious stones, gold...

He took the bundle and placed it at the feet of a Yogi and said, "*Swamiji*, I am placing all my wealth at your feet. I don't need them any more. I only seek peace of mind and happiness. Where is peace?" Saying thus, he fell at the feet of the Yogi in total surrender.

The Yogi did not seem to heed his words at all. He hurriedly opened the bundle, and checked the contents. It was full of dazzling diamonds and glittering gold. On viewing these, the Yogi tied up the bundle and ran away with it.

The rich man was extremely shocked. "Oh no, I have surrendered my wealth to a cheat, a pseudo Godman. What a blunder!" He thought. His sadness turned into anger and he went behind the Yogi in hot pursuit.

The Yogi was unable to run fast. He went into all the lanes and bylanes but finally reached the place from where he had started his run... under the tree. The rich man also reached the same place, panting hard. Before he could utter a word, the Yogi said, "Hey, did you get scared that I would abscond with your wealth? Here, take it, I have no need for it...keep it for yourself," and returned the bundle to him.

The rich man was very happy that he had got back his "lost wealth". "Here is peace," said the Yogi. The Yogi further added, "You see, all this wealth was with you even before you came here, but you did not derive joy from them. It is the same wealth that is with you now but you have found a great joy in your heart. So where did the happiness come from. From wealth or from within you?"

It is clear from the story that joy and happiness are not outside us. They are within us.

"The kingdom of heaven is within you," says the Bible.

Just like the rich man who went roaming around with the bundle of wealth, many of us do not realize this truth. That is the reason why we look up to others for our happiness.

Use Your Third Eye For Happiness in Life

True and lasting happiness will come into your life the day you get the clear realization that you can overcome any weakness.

The day you realize that you have hidden potentials to solve your problems and heal your body, you can prosper yourself beyond your fondest dream. You may have been very happy when you became engaged to the partner of your dreams. You may have felt happy when you graduated from college, when you got married, when your child was born or when you won a great victory, or a prize. You could go on and list other experiences that have made you happy. However, no matter how massive these experiences are, they do not give real lasting happiness. **They are transitory happiness.**

When you trust in God to lead, guide, govern and direct all your ways, you will become poised, serene and relaxed. As you radiate love, peace and goodwill to all, you are really building a superstructure of happiness for all the days of your life.

Happiness is a state of mind. You have the freedom to choose happiness. Many people choose unhappiness without realizing that they are doing so. They do so by entertaining such ideas as:

- *Today is a black day; everything is going to be wrong.*
- *I am not going to succeed.*
- *Everyone is against me.*
- *I never get the breaks.*
- *He can do it I can't and so on.*

If you have this attitude of mind, the first thing in the morning is that you will attract all these experiences to you and be unhappy.

By constantly dwelling on thoughts of fear, worry, anger hate and failure, you will become depressed and unhappy. *Remember, your life is what your thoughts make of it. You cannot buy happiness with all the money in the world.* Some millionaires are happy, some are unhappy. Many people with little worldly wealth are happy and some are unhappy. Some married people are happy and some are unhappy. Some single people are happy and some are unhappy.

"The kingdom of happiness is in your thought and feeling."

Choose Happiness by Your Third Eye

Begin now to choose happiness. That is how you do it. When you open your eyes in the morning, visualise by your third eye by saying to yourself as follows:

"Divine order takes charge of my life today and every day. All things work together for the good of me today. This is a new and wonderful day for me. There will never be another day like this one. I am divinely guided all day long, and whatever I do will prosper. Divine love surrounds me and enwraps me, and I go forth in peace.

Whenever my attention wanders away from that which is good and constructive, I will immediately bring it back to the contemplation of that which is lovely and of good report. I am a spiritual and mental magnet attracting to myself all things that bless and prosper me. I am going to be a wonderful success in all my undertakings today. I am definitely going to be happy all day long."

Another seed of happiness is the way we look at life.

Reflect on the following story: A lady celebrated by dancing three hours in a pub. After dance, she was very happy. As she was taking coffee, coffee spilt on her beautiful saree. Immediately, she screamed saying that her joy of the three hour dance was gone.

Those three hours of happiness were invalidated by a sorrow lasting for a few seconds. If our mind can work like this, the reverse is also possible. **The three hours of sorrow can get invalidated by a few seconds of joy. That is:**

* **The secret of being happy is to recollect happy incidents in life and heighten joy.**
* **When unhappy, weaken its effect by distancing its pictures and not identifying with it. That is why there is urgent need to**

a. **Understand the mind** – That is about thought patterns, values and belief systems, attitudes and opinions.
b. **Transform the mind** – That means:
   i. There is no complete satisfaction in life; there is a possibility to improve upon.
   ii. We don't have to win every time in order to be happy. Happiness does not depend only on success. **Success is a journey and not the destination.**
   iii. Learn to respond and not to react in life.
c. **Transcend the mind** – That means
   i. **To elevate our thoughts system** beyond this physical realm.
   ii. **To nurture the basic values and virtues** in its consciousness.
   iii. **To feel being in an ever happy and blissful state of mind** in all circumstances.

I–INTEGRATE YOUR PERSONALITY

INTEGRATED PERSONALITY

Integrated personality means a balanced, complete, perfect and whole personality. This is a complete positive and powerful personality. In Srimad Bhagwat Geeta, God has defined this personality at "STHITPRAGYA" which means the one who has complete knowledge of the cyclic pattern of the universal planned drama that consists of happiness and sorrow, day and night, hot and cold, ups and downs and so on. Knowing all this he is stable. His consciousness is filled with emotional balance and his state of mind is stable despite contradictions.

"Self-realization is the key of integrated personality."

Life is not just a bed of roses; it has thorns in it too. Thorns act like deterrent.

The people around us can be easily classified into **three different groups.**

In the first group, there are people who say that they will always be with you, irrespective of your good or bad phase. To them, it does not make any difference whether you are successful or a struggler. It is this group of people that makes you believe that you will never be alone.

In the second group, there are people who let you know where you are going wrong. It is this group of people that makes sure that you make fewer mistakes per day. These people tell you to be more careful and thoughtful before taking any decision.

In the third group, there are people who have given you mute consent that they will be with you as long as you are good and successful. These are the people who salute the rising sun. It is people of this group who cause me to leap forward and be the best in whatever I do.

Together, these three diamonds make up the costliest ornament that you can possess. They all contribute to make you a complete and composed person. Like they say, "life is not just a bed of roses, it has thorns in it too."

Practice spirituality in your daily life to integrate your personality

Spirituality or soul-consciousness sets in motion the manifestation of the core virtues/attributes in the form of values in life as follows:

Knowledge /wisdom: We manifest knowledge and wisdom in the form of understanding, maturity, adaptability, balance, discernment, freedom, faith, greatness, humility, manners, punctuality, readiness, self respect, self confidence, fairness, justice, maturity, discipline, farsightedness, introspection, detachment and so on.

Purity: We manifest purity in the form of non violence, truth, honesty, integrity, sincerity, openness, cleanliness, transparency, reality, royalty, courtesy, accuracy, orderliness and so on.

Peace: We manifest peace in the form of coolness, calmness, tolerance, easiness, patience, gentleness, introversion, lightness, positivity, silence and simplicity.

Love: We manifest love in the form of respect, regard, share, care, sacrifice, service, compassion, kindness, cooperation, generosity, mercy, appreciation, benevolence, goodwill, politeness and so on.

Bliss: We manifest bliss in the form of enthusiasm, zeal, pleasantness, unity, cheerfulness, contentment, sweetness and so on.

Happiness: We project happiness in the form of elevation, encouragement, worthiness, lightness, joy, creativity, self confidence, enterprising nature, venturesome nature and so on.

Power: We project power in the form of courage, stability, determination, bravery, constancy, decisiveness, faith, perseverance, fearlessness, tirelessness and so on.

These are the natural qualities / attributes which are the very fabric of the spirit – the soul. These are basically the fundamental principles governing universal welfare and harmony.

Therefore, spirituality means having a lot of spirit in one's life. But what we find is that even though an individual is a spirit, there is no spirit in the spirit that means there is no enthusiasm, zeal, creativity, self-confidence, courage so on and so forth.

Have Faith in God to Develop Power to Face Any Challenge in Your Life

Mullah Nasruddin was married just that morning. The same night, he and his wife were travelling in a boat across a river, along with their relatives.

A sudden storm broke out and the river was turbulent. The boat rocked wildly. Everyone in the boat, including the bride, was in mortal fear. But Mullah Nasruddin remained calm. The bride noticed this and asked in surprise, "Aren't you afraid?" Mullah, without replying took out the dagger from his waistband and raised it as though he was going to slit her throat. There was no reaction on her face. He asked, "Are you not afraid of the dagger?" She said, "The dagger may be dangerous, but the person who is holding it, is my loving husband. So I am not afraid." Exactly exclaimed Mullah, "These waves may be dangerous but Allah who is moving them is full of love. So I am not afraid."

Mullah Nasrudin had faith in Allah. Hence, he loved all and was compassionate. Without faith in God, he would have been devoid of love and compassion. Without love and compassion even Mullah would have trembled with fright just like the others in the boat.

We can apply this example to our lives too. If we are afraid of God, it only means that we do not trust his existence. We would have come across many who say, " I am God fearing. This is nonsense. We should love god, not fear him. *It should be "God loving" not "God fearing."*

Swami Vivekananda said, "Be fearless. Fearlessness is the message of the Upanishads."

Some go from one astrologer to another with their horoscopes to find out when death would strike them. As far as they are concerned, their horoscopes are "horror scopes." Such people are more afraid of when they would die rather than what they would do while being alive. This fear devastates them both mentally and physically.

Instead of conjuring images of fearful events like, "what if I fail in the examination?," and thus spending time weakening yourself, use it fruitfully to prepare and pass in the examination. *Life is a series of examinations: we need to pass them with flying colours. This is a gift we can offer to God.*

J – JEALOUSY REMOVAL

Don't feel jealous about others instead churn the gems of spiritual wisdom. *Jealousy burns our mind and heart, thus blocking heart chakra.* But the spiritual wisdom will bring you solace, comfort and satisfaction. Jealousy exists when one has not learnt to rejoice in the success of others. *Jealousy is the jungle of comparison.*

Rejoice Uniqueness, Not Comparision and Jealousy

Reflect on the following stories: *A dog, having lost its way, enters into a forest. It is a scorching sunny day and the heat is intolerable. Not able to find water, the dog wanders all around. Surprisingly, it finds a pond full of water. Tired and thirsty, the dog rushes towards the water. As it bends down to drink, it sees its reflection in the pool. Now, it's thirst* is forgotten and it barks furiously at its own reflection. It becomes very weak and feeble. Just then a wind blows, ruffling the surface of the water, and the reflection disappears in the ripples. Now the dog eagerly drinks the water, as it is able to see the water and not his reflection.

Who prevented the dog from quenching it's thirst? The answer is the dog itself.

We create our own obstacles by unwisely comparing ourselves to others. Comparing ourselves to a neighbour's possessions or a relative's new acquisition blinds many of us from seeing wonderful happenings in our own lives.

A man prays, "Oh Lord, please fulfill my prayers. I will forever be grateful to you."

The Lord advises, "Son, the more I fulfill your desires, the more you will be unhappy. Your being lives in unhappiness. Focus on changing the state of your being and not on fulfilling of your desires."

But the man insists that his desires be fulfilled. Instead of changing himself he tries to change the Lord. The Lord answered, "I will fulfill your desires but on one condition. Whatever you get, the whole city will get double of it."

The man happily agreed. He prays for a palatial house and next moment finds one. He was very happy. But it was momentary and vanishes as sooner as he notices two palatial houses in his neighbourhood. This leads to anger and jealousy. He feels that it is his effort that he pleased the Lord, but the others are reaping the rewards. He decides to teach them a lesson.

He prays again, "Oh Lord, please remove one of my eyes." Suddenly he find that others had lost both the eyes. He feels very happy. The very next day he finds the whole town has committed suicide. He experiences a sense of loneliness. The joy of making the whole town blind is short lived, as he has nobody to share his success with.

Problems Arises Due to Comparision

A Zen monk visited a small village. The villagers gathered around him and placed their requests before him, "Please help us get rid of our problems; let our desires be fulfilled", and said, "Only then will our lives be full of joy."

The monk listened to them, silently. The next day, he arranged for a heavenly voice...

"Tomorrow at mid-day a miracle is going to take place in this village. Pack all your problems in an imaginary sack, take it across the river and leave it there. Then, in the same imaginary sack, put everything that you want...gold, jewellery, food... and bring it home. You do this and your desires will materialize."

The villagers were in doubt as to whether this oracle was true or not. However, the voice from the heaven astounded them. They thought they had nothing to lose by following the instructions. If it were true, then they would really get what they wanted and if it were false, any way, it wasn't a big deal. So they decided to do what was told.

Next day, at noon, they all packed their troubles in an imaginary sack and went across the river, left it there and brought back all that they thought would bring them happiness...gold, car, house, jewellary, diamonds....

On their return, they were really stunned. Whatever the oracle had said had come true. The man who wanted a car, found one parked in front of his house. The one, who wished for a palatial house, found that his house had turned into one. They were all so happy. Their joy knew no bounds.

But alas, the joy and celebration lasted for a while. Soon they began to compare themselves with their neighbours ...each one felt the person next door was happier and richer than himself. Now they began to talk amongst themselves to pry out more details. The next moment, they were full of remorse.

"I had asked for a simple chain, while the girl next door had asked for an ornate gold necklace and got it. I had just asked for a house but the man residing opposite had asked for a mansion, we too should have asked for such things. It was a wonderful opportunity, the chance of a lifetime...we let it slip by, foolishly."

Such were the thoughts that occupied their minds. Once again they returned to the monk and piled their complaints in front of him. The village was once again plunged into frustration and discontent.

Don't waste time in expectation from others

A turtle family decided to go on a picnic. Turtles, being naturally slow about things, took seven years to prepare for their outing. Finally, the turtle family left home looking for a suitable place. During the second year of their journey they found a place ideal for them at last. For about six months they cleaned the area, unpacked the picnic basket, and completed the arrangements. Then they discovered that they had forgotten the salt. A picnic without salt would be a disaster, they all agreed. After a lengthy discussion, the youngest turtle was chosen to retrieve the salt from home.

Although he was the fastest of the slow moving turtles, the little turtle whined, cried and wobbled in his shell. He agreed to go on one condition, that no one would eat until he returned. The family consented and the little turtle left.

Three years passed and the little turtle had not returned. Five years... six years... then in the seventh year of his absence, the oldest turtle could no longer contain his hunger. He announced that he was going to eat and began to unwrap a sandwich.

At that point the little turtle suddenly popped out from behind a tree shouting, "See I knew you wouldn't wait. Now I am not going to go and get the salt."

Some of us waste our time waiting for people to live up to our expectations. We are so concerned about what others are doing that we don't do anything ourselves.

K – KNOW YOUR KARMIC ACCOUNTS

In today's scenario people know so many things but they neither know self nor know God and the operations of one's karmic accounts. That is why, people grope in the darkness of ignorance and keep searching for the Supreme (God) in different religions and sects and keep praying to God for material returns in their lives.

Operations of karmic accounts are based on the following principles:

+   Additions in karmic accounts are the result of physical and economic help rendered to the needy.

−   Subtractions from karmic accounts are the results of causing physical and economic harm to others.

X   Multiplications in karmic accounts are the results of mental and emotional support in form of good wishes for all.

÷   Reductions by division in karmic accounts are the results of ill will and bad wishes for others.

Be your own guide in dealing with your karmic accounts

You are your own teacher and guide. Be realistic and reasonable while dealing with inner world and outer world situations to maintain a good balance in your karmic ledger. There is nothing here, which we can call our own. We have not brought anything with us when we came to this world. Every body gets the daily quota for a living. We have to be a light unto ourselves. We should not tread the path of life with the light of others lamp, because when the lamps of others burnout we will be in darkness.

Our thoughts, feelings, emotions, imaginations and visions make up our real world. That world is within each of us. Those who have mental power and clear focus in life can only become the light for others. An ideal is very important in our life.

We must form an ideal, after sustained reasonable and realistic experience based thinking, which can only guide and lead us in the right path.

Learn from all life situations (The law of karma is always reformative and not punitive)

Nothing happens without a reason. What we see and observe in this world are consequences. Just because we do not know the reason let us not brow beat. Let us prepare to accept and adapt.

Problems come to us not to tumble us but to humble us

Accept every situation and people. It is an opportunity for learning and growth. Prepare mentally well in advance for such an attitude and approach to life and life situations.

Law of karma and self-sovereignty: Law of cause and effect or law of karma states that every action has an equivalent reaction. In other words, if your action gives happiness to others you get happiness in return. It is the metaphysical equivalent of Newton's third law which says, "every action has an equal, and opposite reaction."

In the metaphysical plane the reaction or result experienced is equivalent and not opposite. The saying goes, **"As you sow, so shall you reap." The law of karma is absolute.** It cannot be manipulated or side tracked. On the physical level there is no gap between action and reaction or sowing and reaping. The seeds of some actions bring instantaneous results; others can take years or even lifetimes to yield the fruit. What happens in our personal world and the world at large are the direct result of our actions. The social injustice, inept governments, needless bloodshed, physical pain are the consequences of thoughts, words or deeds of this or other lives on a personal or collective level.

Settlement of Karmic Debts

- Every human being is an actor on this stage of life; each one is playing his or her respective role. If a person is behaving badly with us it is because we have to settle our previous karmic accounts with that soul.
- There lies something beneficial in every scene of this drama; every scene is a teacher, a test paper that we need to pass in order to move ahead in life. If we are facing tough situations, we are merely settling old karmic accounts and these are lessening our burden. On a higher vista of consciousness, you begin to view the arrival of an unpleasant occurrence in your life as the challenge that it was intended to be.

Challenges are designed, at a soul level, to give rise to change. Change then opens the door to the opportunity for transformation, and transformation is our main purpose of life.

Your soul thinks very much in terms of service to others, so your purpose in life is to transform, not only yourself, but also all of humanity to a higher level of consciousness. As a member of the group and the mind of humanity on the earth, everything that you do is reflected within the whole. Many challenges are undertaken; more for the transformation that they will bring to others, than for the change they will bring to you.

Transformation itself is the natural progress of the spirit, which can be effortless. But when a blockage to that transformation exists, pain may be the price necessary to dissolve that blockage. People often take on pain in their lives, not because their souls see that society needs to work through certain major issues but because they volunteer to be a part of that transformation.

In some people's lives, challenges come thick and fast. In others, they do not, at least for that lifetime. When a person completes a particularly challenging lifetime, they may follow it up with a quiet, pleasant and restful incarnation, one where nothing outstanding happens at all.

Without that tension in life, nothing moves and nothing progresses. Huge issues are worked through by millions of people at a time. Take any issue equality of the sexes, equality of race, control issues, abuse, violence, equal access for the handicapped and there are millions of people working through each issue at any one time in history.

Sometimes people make obvious progress in helping shift the paradigm. Sometimes they pass away before their time, a seeming victim of the old reality, having made no apparent progress. However, whatever they do in their lives, the experience of just being alive in their situation is added to the massive paradigm shift in consciousness, which is occurring at that time. No effort is wasted. No one fails. Everyone contributes to the experiences, which follow each challenge.

Not all challenges in life are a part of massive society shifts. A challenge may just as easily be personal. Something is perhaps chosen as a tool to break up a long-standing blockage within a person's psyche. *It is almost surreal to hear a cancer survivor reflect on his newfound health and say, "Cancer was the best thing that had ever happened to me." What he mean is that the challenge transformed him by releasing old blockages, which were cheating him of a fuller life.*

We may never know all of the reasons why bad events happen. What we do know is that, in a world, which habitually contrasts light and dark, the events, which appear bad, can often be the greatest opportunities for transformation within ourselves, for those around us and for humanity as a whole.

- **Coincidences are God's way of remaining anonoymous.**
  (Doris Lessing)
- **In asking for miracles, we are not asking for something outside us to change, but for something inside us to change.** (Marianne Williamson)

As you sow, so shall you reap

Here is the story (A true story from Associated Press, reported by Kurt Wester), which proves how a karmic debt is settled by natural coincidence. It is the result of one's actions.

At the 1994 Annual Awards dinner given for Forensic Sciences in the USA, AAFS President Dr Don Harper Mills astounded his audience with the legal complications of a bizarre death.

On 23 March 1994, the medical examiner viewed the body of Ronald Opus and concluded that he had died from a shotgun wound in the head. Mr Opus had jumped from the top of a ten-storey building intending to commit suicide. He had left a note to the effect, indicating his despondency. As he fell past the ninth floor his life was interrupted by a shotgun blast passing through a window, which killed him instantly.

Neither the shooter nor the deceased was aware that a safety net had been installed just below the eighth floor level to protect some building workers and that Ronald Opus would not have been able to complete his suicide the way he had planned. "Ordinarily," Dr Mills continued, "a person who sets out to commit suicide and ultimately achieves what he intended, is still defined as committing suicide." That Mr Opus was shot on the way to certain death, but probably would not have been successful because of the safety net, caused the medical examiner to feel that he had a homicide on his hands.

An elderly man and his wife occupied the room on the ninth floor from where the shotgun blast emanated. They were arguing vigorously and he was threatening her with a shotgun. The man was so upset that when he pulled the trigger he completely missed his wife and the bullet went through the window, striking Mr Opus. When one intends to kill subject 'A' but kills subject 'B' in the attempt, one is guilty of the murder of subject 'B'. When confronted with the murder charge, the old man and his wife were both adamant and both said that they thought the shotgun was unloaded. The old man said it was a long-standing habit to threaten his wife with the unloaded shotgun. He had no intention of murdering her. Therefore, the killing of Mr Opus appeared to be an accident; that the gun had been accidentally loaded. The continuing investigation turned up a witness who saw the old couple's son loading the shotgun about six weeks prior to the fatal accident. It transpired that the old lady had cut off her son's financial support and the son, knowing the propensity of his father to use the shotgun threateningly, loaded the gun with the expectation that his father would shoot his mother. Since the loader of the gun was aware of this, he was guilty of the murder even though he didn't actually pull the trigger. The case now becomes one of murder on the part of the son for the death of Ronald Opus.

Now comes the exquisite twist. Further investigation revealed that the son was in fact, Ronald Opus. He had become increasingly despondent over the failure of his attempt to engineer his mother's murder. This led him to jump off the tenth storey building on March 23, only to be killed by a shotgun blast passing through the ninth storey window. The son had actually murdered himself, so the medical examiner closed the case as a suicide.

L – LOVE ALL AND LAUGH FROM HEART

Love is LIFE (Love – an Infinite – Flow – of pure Energy). LOVE is Life of Vast Energy. Here love is a positive spiritual energy. Everyone on this earth radiates it. It is pure and warm. It purifies the soul that is why it is said *"flow the Ganga of Love by delighting the souls on the earth"*.

Don't confuse love with lust. *Lust is impure and carries negative energy.* It is disliked and said, "fallen in love (lust)". But there is no fall, only "rise in pure love". Pure love is a bond of spiritual energy, which binds all relations and religions in one thread.

Once a beggar who lived under a tree died. A year later, when the land was being ploughed, workers found treasure of money, rubies, diamonds buried beneath the spot where the beggar lived.

*Adi Shankaracharya pointed out that most of us, like the beggar, are seated on great treasures. **There is a treasure of love, joy and silence within us but our worrying mind makes us live like beggars.** We are forgetful. Remind yourself that you are not a beggar.*

God loves those who love others

Abu Ben Adham was an ordinary man who used to spend his time and energy in serving his community and society at large. He was a philanthropist (lover of mankind). One day, when he got up from his sleep, he saw the sun's rays falling into his room. As he watched, he saw an angel emerge out of the light. The angel was carrying a very big book with him.

Surprised, Abu asked, "Angel, why are you here and what is that big book you are carrying?"

The angel smiled and said, "I came here to show you this big book. This one carries the names of the people who love God."

Abu inquisitively asked, "Can you please check, whether my name is there?"

The angel checked all the pages but Abu's name was not there. Abu was disappointed but remarked philosophically, "I understand that I never went to any temple, I never gave any money as donation to any house of God, however all my life, I have served poor people, helped the needy and the underprivileged. It is no surprise that my name is not there in the list."

On hearing this, the angel said, "Wait a minute, and pulled out a small scribbling pad from his coat pocket. Abu asked what it was. The angel smiled and said, "Oh, this book? This contains the names of those few people whom God loves. Let me see if your name is there in this list."

As the angel opened the small book, the first name on the first page was that of Abu Ben Adham.

We may go to a temple everyday, we may pray to God everyday, we might worship him every second. Yes, we all might love God. But this does not mean that the God loves us too. **However, if we love and serve our fellow human beings and help them out, take care of the people around us and love them wholeheartedly, God will sure, love us.**

So in which book would you like your name to be? In the majority list of people who love God or In the minority list of people whom the God loves? **Decide and start spreading the love for all human beings. Change your thoughts and you change your world.**

Love brings wealth and success

A woman came out of her house and saw three old men with long white beards sitting in her front yard. She did not recognize them. She said, "I don't think I know you, but you must be hungry. Please come in and have something to eat."

"Is the man of the house at home?" they asked.

"No," she replied. "He is out."

"Then we cannot come in," they replied.

In the evening when her husband came home, she told him what had happened.

"Go, tell them that I am at home and invite them in."

The woman went out and invited the men in. "We do not go into a house together," they replied.

"Why is that?" she asked.

One of the old men explained: "His name is Wealth," he said pointing to one of his friends and said pointing to the other one, "He is Success, and I am Love." Then he added, "Now go in and discuss with your husband which one of us you want in your home."

The woman went in and told her husband what was said. Her husband was overjoyed. "How nice!" he said, "since that is the case, let us invite Wealth. Let him come and fill our home with Wealth!"

His wife disagreed. "My dear, why don't we invite Success?"

Their daughter-in-law was listening from the other corner of the house. She jumped in with her own suggestion: "Would it not be better to invite Love? Our home will then be filled with love!"

"Let us heed our daughter-in-law's advice," said the husband to his wife.

"Go out and invite Love to be our guest."

The woman went out and asked the three old men, "Which one of you is Love? Please come in and be our guest."

Love got up and started walking toward the house. The other two also got up and followed him. Surprised, the lady asked Wealth and Success: "I only invited Love, why are you coming in?"

The old men replied together: "If you had invited Wealth or Success, the other two of us would've stayed out, but since you invited Love, wherever he goes, we go with him. Wherever there is Love, there is also Wealth and Success."

Laughter is A Godly Gift, Laugh to Remain Healthy

Laughter is a Godly gift given to human beings. It is one of the blessings that differentiate us from rest of the animal kingdom. As human beings, we come across so much stress and tension because of our unplanned and hectic schedule. To substantiate our energy levels to meet the urgent requirements, to fulfill time bound tasks, our body undergoes a certain amount of stress. *But after completion of that particular time bound task, some of that un-consumed stress (power) settles inside the body, and transforms into toxins (poisons) and keep accumulating.* Over a period of time, this accumulated stress can lead to **cancer, high blood pressure, diabetes and other lifestyle related diseases and disorders.** It is proven that laughter is the best method to maintain optimum stress levels, and it helps to prevent major health problems.

Laughter enhances immunity power. It raises the levels of cells that fight with infection. Laughter assists in conflict management. It also helps in reducing anger, makes you optimistic, adds joy and helps you build a positive attitude.

Laugh Your Way to the Treasure of Health and Wealth

Laughter does amazing things for you. *A good laugh straight from your belly can actually give you an aerobic workout.* And humour in the work place enhances team building. If you don't have a rowing machine, don't worry, just laugh a 100 times, because laughing that many times is equivalent to 10 minutes on a rowing machine, and you can lose weight in an easy, pleasant way.

Laughing maintains blood pressure and raises vascular blood flow. It also assists in the oxygeneration of blood. A hearty laugh exercises the diaphragm as well as abdominal, respiratory and facial muscles. At work, laughter helps you solving problems creatively, because it employs many of the skills used in problem solving.

Laughter improves communication skills and team building. If you laugh 17 times a day, then you are normal. An average adult laughs that many times a day. If not, it is time you form a group and start laughing without reason. It may seem odd at first but it is a fantastic stress buster. Over time, you will learn to love it.

Message of Laughing Buddha – Smile and Laugh

You might have heard of the "Laughing Buddha". There were three Buddhist monks – just as Buddha got enlightened under the Bodhi tree, these three monks also got enlightened through laughter. They later taught the world that laughing could be a way of meditation. They spread the message of laughter throughout their lives, far and wide.

One of the monks passed away. The other two sat on either side of his body and began to laugh. The town people were angered by this seemingly inappropriate behaviour and started abusing them. To this, the monks replied:

"Our friend spent his whole life in helping people to understand the message of laughter. We are laughing because

- *He has won the game of death*
- *The message from his life was laughter*
- *If we do not bid him farewell with laughter his soul will laugh at us that we are trapped like others by seriousness.*

Thus, we are laughing, as per his wish before his death."

It was time to conduct the final rites for the funeral. The monk had said before his death, "Since I was laughing throughout my life, laughter has cleansed all impurities from within me. So please do not wash my body with water."

Accordingly, his body was not bathed, but taken directly to the funeral pyre. As the body was lit by fire, suddenly there was a burst of crackers from the pyre. Yes! The monk had fastened crackers to his body under his flowing robes before his death. He had done so to make every one laugh even after his death! Hence he was called the "Laughing Buddha".

There is no better cosmetic than a genuine smile!

Apply any amount of cosmetics as you wish to. Face powder, eye shadow and lipstick to enhance your beauty…. but would they all become equal to one genuine smile?

If two barely acquainted persons, meet and laugh at some jokes… chances are that they would become good friends!

Not only does laughter fetch you new friends,
but it also strengthens old friendships.

M – MANAGE YOUR ANGER

Anger is undoubtedly a self-defeating and self-destructive emotion. It can cause physical problems like disturbed sleep, tiredness, hypertension, heart problems, ulcers, stiffness in the joints and other physical complications. Expression of hostile anger is also destructive to relationships, leading to guilty feelings and self- directed anger for causing hurt and pain to others and also isolation and alienation from others due to the damages in relationships. These in turn lead to immense loneliness and extreme mental and emotional anguish, leading to depression, which can sometimes end in suicide.

Anger, when out of control, can lead to violence against someone you are close to, leading to physical injury and even fatalities. You may say or do things that you cannot undo.

Relationships get damaged, sometimes irreversibly the victim may either retaliate or withdraw, giving in to the fight or flight impulse. In either case, the relationship suffers, as the relationship finishes at the emotional level.

ANGER IS A DANGER
ANGER IS A SELF PARALYSING EMOTION
ANGER AFFECTS ONE'S MIND AND BODY
ADVERSELY
ANGER IS A TEMPORARY MADNESS
ANGER HARMS YOU FIRST, THEN OTHERS.

Forms of Anger

Impatience: It is one of the forms of anger in which a person become impatient. He is in the habit of doing things fast. Any interruption causes anger and creates stress. For example – waiting at road crossing during red light etc.

Irritability: It is one of the forms of anger in which a person is in the habit of getting irritated about trifles either at home or elsewhere. For example – TV remote stops working, items are not placed at the right places etc.

Frustration: It is one of the forms of anger in which a person is in the habit of getting frustrated at every minor failure or at the things or situations not taking place as per his choice or desires. Frustration by itself does not cause anger, it is the way we view the frustration that causes anger. Extreme anger results when things don't happen the way we want them to, and believe that they 'should' happen. It is our irrational belief that is 'demanding' that we 'should' have our way, so we view it as 'awful' and 'unbearable' if we don't have our way and that cause anger. For example – if our Indian team loses a match, not getting one's proper share or remuneration etc.

Indignation: It is one of the forms of anger in which a person expresses or suppresses his indignation if he is not given due recognition or if his desires remain unfulfilled. For example – if we feel we are ignored or not appreciated etc.

Self-righteousness: It is one of the forms of anger in which a person feels that he is always right and asserts it in every situation. If the things are not taking place as per his preferences or directives, he expresses his anger and asserts himself without knowing the causes or consequences of it. For example – if someone arrives late, a job is not completed in time etc.

Fury: It is the worst form of anger, which is a result of accumulated unexpected anger, which has been bottled up because of the fear of confrontation. This bottling up results in a disproportionate blow-up and the conflict, which was being avoided so far, is unleashed in a manner that is shocking for the one who blows up and also for the one at the receiving end.

Depending upon the situations anger is either suppressed or expressed.

Causes of Anger

There may be following causes of anger –
* Unfulfilled desires and expectation
* Ego and self-centredness
* Discontentment
* Low self-esteem
* Lack of self control
* Ignorance of 'True' self or body consciousness

Now reflect on the following story:

A husband never bothered about the likes and dislikes of his wife. The wife's reciprocal attitude perfectly suited her husband. One night, the husband had not returned home till midnight. The wife, not worried about him, had long since retired to bed. In the middle of the night, there was a knock at the door. The wife opened the door. It was her husband. He had brought a monkey along with him. As soon as she saw the monkey, the wife was furious. However, she swallowed her anger and went to bed. He placed the monkey on the bed between him and his wife.

Now she could not contain her anger any more. "How can you let a monkey sleep by my side? How can I bear this nuisance and nasty smell?"

"Haven't I got used to your foul smell ever since I married you? So, soon this monkey too would get used to it." said the husband. These pricking words hurt the wife. On the same night, their marital life came to an end.

Here 'monkey' is a mnemonic keyword or a metaphor representing ill will and vicious and non-compromising attitude instead of a loving, smiling and accommodating attitude, which could have strengthened their relation instead of breaking it apart.

Effects of Anger

Anger plays havoc with your responsibility. The effects of anger are as follows –

- *Pushes back qualities*
- *Sours relationship*
- *Brings disrespect*
- *Blocks co-operation*
- *Takes away happiness*
- *Ends in repentance*
- *Depletes energy*
- *Clouds judgement*

- *Causes emotional imbalance*
- *Results in irritable nature*
- *Leads to unbecoming conduct*

NOW VISUALISE ABOVE WRITTEN EFFECTS OF ANGER IN YOUR OWN LIVING ENVIRONMENT AND FIND OUT WHAT YOU ARE LOSING OUT DUE TO ANGER

Now reflect on the following story: The house is in darkness. Out of anger, if one enters it, one is bound to tumble on various items of furniture. Getting annoyed or throwing the furniture out of the house is not the solution. The reason for the fall is not the furniture, but the darkness. So what has to be thrown out is not the furniture. Once we light the lamp, darkness will disappear and so too will the problems. There was a noble tailor, who had transformed himself into a great sage.

The king came to pay his obeisance. The king gifted him golden scissors, encrusted with diamonds. But the sage refused to accept it. The king was worried that he was not able to help the sage. So he asked him, "What can I give that would be of use to you?"

The sage replied, "Give me a needle."

The king at once arranged for a needle and presented it to the sage. Humbly, he waited for the sage's response. The sage said, "The reason why I refused your gift of scissors is because it cuts and divides."

Our minds are like scissors that cut and divide. But the needle will stitch, join and unite. Our hearts are like needles which join and unite.

Today, humanity is in need of a needle and not scissors.
SO LIGHT THE LAMP OF KNOWLEDGE & TRUTH IN YOU AND PRICK THE NEEDLE GENTLY WITH LOVE AND BEST WISHES TO STITCH THE DIVIDED HUMANITY

Managing Anger with Four Steps

To manage your anger, do the following –

1. **Develop unconditional love**: Life is like a musical instrument. Tradition and relationship are the two aspects of life.

If you keep tradition aside for a while and focus on enhancing a relationship, the music that emanates from life will be wonderful. Well, what is the way for a husband and wife to live without quarrels and squabbles – in other words, in perfect understanding of each other?

The first requirement is unconditional love.

Negative feelings like anger, self-pity, and guilt... reside in our nervous system. At any given opportunity, these feelings will vent out with great force without our awareness. These are known as '**Energy Clots**'. Just like a bomb that bursts after a flame touches its wick, these clots break up like an earthquake, due to use of certain sensitive words. They can even burn the relationship of love and understanding that is as cool as ice. So, please avoid using words that can make your spouse burst.

When a child begins to walk, he can be quite unsteady. At times, he can fall. When he falls, if the parents are not nearby, he would just pick himself up and walk on. On the other hand, if he falls in the presence of his parents, he would wail loud enough to gather the whole neighbourhood. Thus, his racket is to seek attention. Sometimes even grown-ups have this characteristic.

Every husband or wife craves for attention from the other. So be sensitive to this reality and handle such situations with maturity by giving meaningful attention. If one fails in doing this, their mental games while seeking attention manipulatively will go on.

2. Develop inter-personal communication skill: Recently, a reputed university in USA conducted a survey to analyse the characteristics of persons who rise quickly in their professional life.

Do you know the result of this survey?

For a person to succeed in his profession, 35 percent subject knowledge is sufficient, but what is important is, 65 percent knowledge about interpersonal skills. That is to say, only a person, who knows how to strengthen relationships, can surpass any barriers to grow and come up in his profession. If the skills for strengthening relationship are necessary at the workplace where one works for monetary returns, then can you imagine how important they are at home too?

Even if a person has made a mistake, do not tell him, "What you have done is wrong". On the contrary, help him see what is right rather than make him feel wrong. Even if you have to criticize someone apply the sandwich technique.... Place your criticism between praises. There are many communication skills like disarming, pre-emptive strikes, multiple closes, emptying technique.

Communication is an art. Art cannot be taught but it has to be caught. The best way to learn communication is to be with people who are good at it. Words can build bridges and walls as well. We have to learn to build bridges.

Very often we find that we have not learnt the art of using appropriate words and we land in trouble. But if one has mastered this art, one can easily overcome problems in communication.

Reflect on this story: There was a debate between the Goddess of Fortune and God of Misfortune to settle who amongst them was more beautiful. They decided to find out the same from a third person. They chose to meet a woman for an apt judgment. The woman they met was in a dilemma. If she were to judge the Goddess of Fortune as beautiful, then the God of Misfortune would invade her life and the other way round, the Goddess of Fortune could forsake her. She therefore asked for sometime on the pretext that she had to say her prayers before the judgement, so as to invoke her God for assistance.

The woman said, "Both of you re-enter my house and leave after a while." The Goddess and God were puzzled... what a way to invite. They however, did what the woman wanted.

The woman gave her judgement. She said, "The Goddess of Fortune appears more beautiful while entering the house and the God of Misfortune appears more beautiful while leaving the house."

This statement is true and at the same time tactful. This is called linguistic intelligence.

The following points are important in the field of communication–

* *Feel good about yourself.*
* *Do not be a victim to impress others, instead express yourself.*
* *Learn to avoid using 'I' and 'Me' instead use 'You' and 'We'.*
* *Learn to make the other person comfortable in your presence.*
* *Practice – pause, pace, pitch and voice modulation while speaking.*
* *Learn to adopt emptying technique while convincing others.*

Emptying technique involves asking questions in such a way as to empty the others while bringing out their likes and dislikes. This would give us a picture of what other wants, so that we can represent our communication in an accommodating climate.

Practice the 'Soften' Technique: While socializing find out who among the strangers are having:

S – Smiling

O – Open body posture

F – Friendly energy

T – Touching while talking

E – Eye Contact

N – Nodding in affirmation

Then strike a conversation with those who have such qualities. Invariably you will feel comfortable with them. According to yoga, there are three types of logic in communication –

* *Tarka – just an cold logic without a context.*
* *Ku Tarka – logic, which always justifies and protects one's point of view.*
* *Vi Tarka – logic, which emphasises having a breakthrough and not focusing on a breakdown.*

During communication, if one adopts *Vi Tarka*, the words will be empowering and not overpowering.

Whenever, there is a conflict in relationship, learn to present and not thrust your point of view.

Let love be your centre while communicating. You will understand the other better rather than feeling bitter.

Though healthy communication is the way to defuse hostilities, it sometimes can be hard to think rationally when anger is getting out of control.

To help in such times, here is a checklist of the systematic steps –

Remember 6 'A's as follow–

- *Be Aware of your anger*
- *Admit that it is irrational*
- *Acknowledge the role you play in creating it*
- *Avoid self-condemnation*
- *Accept responsibility for changing it and*
- *Take Action to change it.*

Remember 7 'C's to improve better relationship:

a. Careful consideration: When you meet the person of your dreams, please calm yourself down long enough to listen to everything your partner says and assess its possible impact on your relationship. Carefully consider all aspects of your partner's character, words and behaviour so that you can make balanced (mental as well as emotional) choices about love.

b. Calm: In the midst of a spirited disagreement, take the time to count till 20 (or 100 if you need to) to calm yourself down and maintain your composure.

c. Courtesy: 'Please', 'would you mind', 'excuse me', and 'thank you', are important phrases to use freely at home as well as with the general public. During discussions express your thoughts; ask for what you want, and then give the floor over to your partner to respond and listen.

d. Co-operation: In the spirit of co-operation, the couple agree to respect each other, to avoid calling each other names and bringing up old stuff that has nothing to do with the situation at hand.

e. Call: Call to say 'Hello' from work. Call to say "I was thinking about how much I love you." Call to say 'I' will be late. Call to give advance notice that you are bringing home a guest. Call to ask if there is anything needed from the market.

f. Commitment: Commit to identifying a solution that works for the relationship. Your goal is to have a long term, happy union, which may at times mean you have to concede a few points and find a middle ground.

g. Compromise: You give something to get something. You exchange desires sometimes because it makes your partner happy. It is good for your relationship or marriage, so you do it without keeping tabs.

3. Wear your helmet according to your role: Wearing helmet here means changing mentality according to one's role and relationships. You may be a father/mother, brother/sister, son/daughter, wife/husband, friend, employer/employee, superior/subordinate and so on. If you wear the mentality of a boss in office at your home, you can imagine what will happen. Home is the heart of human beings where only love resides whereas office is a place where law and cooperation exist together. As environment changes so your role too changes. Be what you are supposed to be in that particular environment.

4. Build the best: An elderly master mason in China named Mo was ready to retire. The contractor was sorry to see his good worker go and asked if he could build just one more house as a personal favour.

Mo said yes, but in time it was easy to see that his heart was not in his work. He resorted to shoddy workmanship and used inferior materials.

When the contractor came to inspect the finished house, he handed the front-door key to Mo. " This is your house," he said, " my gift to you."

What a shock! What a shame! Had Mo known he was building his own house, he would have done it all so differently. Now he had to live in the house he had built very badly.

Think of yourself as the mason of your life. Each day you hammer a nail, place a board, or erect a wall. Build wisely. It is the only life you will ever build. Even if you live it for only one day more, that day deserves to be lived graciously and with dignity. The plaque on the wall says, "Life is a do-it-yourself project". Your life tomorrow will be the result of your attitudes and the choices you make today.

Create the echo of life: A son and his father were walking on the mountains. Suddenly his son fell, hurt himself and screamed: AAAhhhhhhhh

To his surprise, he heard the voice repeating, somewhere in the mountain, AAAhhhhh

Curious, he yelled: "Who are you?"

He received the answer: "Who are you?"

Angered at the response, he screamed: "Coward."

He received the answer: "Coward."

He looked to his father and asked; "What's going on?"

The father smiled and said: "My son, pay attention."

Then he screamed to the mountain; "I admire you."

The voice answered: "I admire you."

Again the man screamed: "You are a champion."

The voice answered: "You are a champion."

The boy was surprised, but did not understand. Then the father explained:

"People call this ECHO, but really this is LIFE. It gives back everything you say or do. Our life is simply a reflection of our actions. If you want more love in the world, create more love in your heart. If you want more competence in your team, improve your competence. This relationship applies to everything, in all aspects of life. Life will give you back everything you have given to it."

Your life is not a coincidence. It is a reflection of you.

Overcoming Anger Completely

Pay attention to the following points to overcome anger completely. There is a great difference between overcoming anger and managing anger. Overcoming anger means programming one's mind with peace and telling bye-bye to anger forever. Managing anger means controlling self from losing temper and avoiding consequences of anger.

* *Practicing moderation*
* *Keeping balance in life. For example – keeping balance between love and law, balance between rights and duties etc.*
* *Practicing control over emotions*
* *Positive Thinking and Being well wisher of all "Shubh Bhavna & Shubh Kamna"*
* *Understanding the drama of life*
* *Understanding the law of karma*
* *Thinking of world as a family (think globally and act locally)*
* *Attitudinal change*
* *Determination to give up anger*
* *Paying attention i.e. is carefully watching over thoughts, words and deeds.*
* *Regular checking for change, being angry on anger.*
* **Practice Rajyoga Meditation for achieving the above objectives**

Proact But Donot React In Anger

"I get angry, when scolded in public.

I get angry, when my colleague blunders.

I get angry, when spoken of, behind my back"

The list is endless. Let us stop here and focus at anger and understand what it is.

When we deem ourselves to be inferior, there is a reaction and it shows up as anger.

When a person calls us "donkey", we retaliate by calling him "monkey". This is reaction.

When we react, external situations control us. In the management lexicon the word used more often is proactive, not reactive.

What is the difference between these two words?

"The following Zen story throws light on this"

There was a Samurai. After winning a war, he was returning home with his army. On the way, he passed through a forest. In the forest, a monk was deep in meditation. The Samurai bowed and asked humbly, "Oh Monk, which is the way to heaven and which is the way to hell?

The monk did not respond. Now the Samurai repeated his question a little more loudly. The monk still did not respond. The third time, the Samurai roared the question in a thunderous voice that shook the very tree under which the monk was meditating. Now the monk opened his eyes and said sternly, "You stupid fellow; why did you disturb my meditation?"

Now the Samurai was really furious. He immediately pulled out his sword and raised it to kill the monk. The monk said with a smile, "This is the way to hell."

The Samurai realised his folly. The truth dawned on him and his anger abated. "The monk called me 'stupid' not to chide me but to teach me the truth all though." He gently placed his sword in the sheath. The monk said, "this is the way to heaven."

When the monk rebuked the Samurai in front of his soldiers, he was angry. "How could this monk rebuke me in front of my soldiers, I have been demeaned; the respect for me is gone. Now how will these fellows show me any regard in the future?" Thus ran his thoughts, lowering his self-esteem, filling him with regret and sorrow. So, he failed to think and drew out his sword – this is "reaction". To react – is the gate to hell.

The reason to call the Samurai stupid was not to belittle him, but to answer his question in an indirect way. The Samurai was quick to grasp the teaching of the monk. Soon the sword found its place in the sheath- this is "pro-action." To respond – is the gate to heaven.

Hell and heaven are the states of mind.

When we get angry with other, we lose our balance. Our blood pressure rises and limbs tremble. For being angry, irrespective of the situation around us, punishment is meted out to us in the form of anger. We are responsible for our state.

N – NO TO WASTE AND NEGATIVE THOUGHTS

Waste and negative thoughts are the root cause of stress. Past is called *"bhoot"* (Ghost) in Hindi. So never lament about Ghost. Don't feel sorry about what you have done yesterday because now yesterday is not in your hands. Yesterday is dead. Also don't worry about tomorrow. Tomorrow is not yet born. ONLY TODAY is in your hands. Put all efforts in making your today positive and successful.

Negative Feeling Clouds Our Consciousness

When one is in a negative frame of mind, observe the following steps:

- Negativity is not in a given situation; it is more in us. For example when we say, "Picnic is spoiled because of rain" a negative feeling is generated – is it in rain or in us?
- Do not identify yourself with negative feelings. *Feelings are like clouds, which come and go fleetingly; but you are like the space.* Do not identify with the clouds; but be centered in the space of consciousness. This process is called detachment. When you are attached to your negative feelings you become a prisoner to them. Attachment creates hell.

Reflect on the following story: In the earlier days, there was an interesting technique for catching monkeys. A huge jar with a narrow neck was used. Nuts were dropped into a narrow necked jar, in the presence of a monkey. A monkey trying to grab the nuts from the jar got caught, because its fist clutching the nuts would get stuck in the narrow necked jar. Only if it dropped the nuts, would its hand be free and easy to remove from the jar. But the monkeys were too attached to the nuts and to drop them free themselves; hence, they were caught.

Are we also attached like this? Can we experience a sense of wonderment when we see difficult people creating their own world of hell? The experience of wonderment relaxes one's being. First change has to happen within us, only then we can motivate others.

"If you feel good, you will experience that the world is right. But ignorant people feel that only if the world is right would they feel good."

Negative Thinking Can Kill You

Nazis' Experiments with Prisoners of War: We are all aware that the Nazis conducted gruesome experiments on prisoners of war. This was one such experiment. They told the prisoners, "We are going to kill you in a novel way. We want to see how you die when the blood in your body is slowly drained away."

As a trial, they put two prisoners in bed and began to drain their blood. The blood was allowed to drain into a nearby bottle making a dripping sound. After a few minutes, they tied their eyes with a black cloth. Then they stopped draining the blood from one of the prisoners' body. But the dripping noise was made to continue, using some other means. The prisoner who was listening to the sound began to tremble in mortal fear. He thought that all the blood was draining from his body, while in reality, it was not so.

"Oh! I am going to die in a short while." he thought. By the end of the experiment, both the prisoners died".

In the case of the first prisoner, the very feeling of his blood oozing out continuously was sufficient to kill him. The reason for death was his mere thoughts impacting his feelings.

A real story: A middle-aged man worked in a refrigeration unit in America. One day, he accidentally locked himself inside. He banged on the door, he yelled and he screamed but no one heard him and finally he accepted his destiny. He sat down, his body became numb and with his fingers he scribbled a message on the wall for those Who would eventually find him. It said: "Getting colder now, starting to shiver, nothing to do but wait, slowly freezing to death, half asleep now these are my final words."

Five hours later they opened the door and found the man dead inside.

That is a sad story, but here is the twist. The temperature inside the unit was low, but not unbearable because the unit had broken down earlier in the day and there was plenty of air for the man to breathe. The man literally willed himself to die.

These stories illustrate the destructive power of the negative thoughts. Your mind cannot distinguish between your thoughts and reality. So if your mind is playing over negative scenarios, it thinks that these are actually happening, as was the case in the example above.

Stop Brooding Over Past (Waste Thoughts)

Suppose your friend comes to you and gives you a video CD of a boring movie that you dislike and sits with you to watch it all through the night, again and again. How would you like it? You would simply be fed-up with boredom. Similarly, the past incidents like the treachery of friends, torture of mother-in-law or daughter-in-law, or by husbands or a nagging wife, all painful scenes of the past that you dislike immensely are just like a boring movie in your memory bank. Then why do you insist on playing them and replaying them over and over again on the mental screen?

While you refuse to watch an imaginary film that you merely dislike and find boring, how can you replay those scenes that you loathe, on your mental screen? Allow yourself to forget them…. the wound will dry up and the scar will vanish by itself.

The reason why small children are always happy is because they do not carry burdens from the past… they forget painful incidents very quickly, but they bring up joyful memories again and again and enjoy them. We too should learn to be like children. That will considerably lessen the burden that we carry in our hearts.

To put all this in a nutshell, the past must only tutor us, not torture us.

In such a space, a hidden intelligence will surface which will guide us in a mysterious way.

For example, tell a person to walk on a road that is two feet wide. He can walk very easily. Let him walk on the two feet wide space that is placed 500 feet high. He will be nervous. Why is it so? Fear and worry erode efficiency.

Similarly, your son has studied well, but at the time of examination – as his mind is filled with worry and fear – he forgets. The answer is to cultivate consciously the spiritual quality of non-worry. Stay calm and focus on the present. Worrying starts when we imagine what will happen if we fail.

This negative autosuggestion should be replaced by positive thoughts. Let the mind say: "I can, I can". The cans create success and can'ts create failure.

Incidentally, we tend to 'forget' the significance of ancient customs and traditions. How many of us know why we break coconuts in the temple? It symbolizes the breaking of the ego. Inside the coconut there is sweet water. When the ego is broken, the sweet water of joy and love emerges. The 'tilak' we draw on the forehead symbolizes the third eye, the eye of intuition.

Consider this real life incident that occurred many years ago in Thailand. An ancient statue of Buddha made of clay, was being shifted to another place. During the journey, it started raining heavily. Some of the helpers covered over the idol with coconut leaves. Still, the idol got wet and the clay started getting washed away. Lo and behold, the disappearing clay revealed a figure of gold. A golden idol had been camouflaged in clay to prevent thieves from stealing it. **This is the story of the golden Buddha in Thailand.**

Covering ourselves with clay, we have 'forgotten' the golden Buddha within us. Catering only to the body, we have neglected the inner self. Worrying is muddying the mind. Our real nature is like the calm, golden Buddha.

Past Events Cause Pain and Affect Our Behaviour

Once, a big monk and a little monk were travelling together. They came to a river bank and found that the bridge was damaged. They had to cross the river. There was also a pretty woman waiting to cross the river, but she was unable to do so. The big monk offered help and carried her across the river on his back. The little monk was shocked by the big monk's offer. "How can he carry a woman when we are supposed to avoid all intimacy with woman?" thought the little monk. But he kept quiet. The big monk carried the woman across the river and the small monk followed unhappily. When they crossed the river, the big monk set the woman down and everybody went their own way.

For the next hour, the little monk remained unhappy with what the big monk had done. He couldn't stop himself from thinking of the audacious act of the big monk. This made him more and more angry, especially since the big monk remained calm and nonchalant and felt no need to explain his actions. Finally, when they stopped to rest many hours later, the little monk burst out and said: " How can you claim to be a devout monk when you seize the first opportunity to touch a woman, especially a very pretty one? All your teachings to me were false. You are a big hypocrite."

The big monk looked surprised and said, "I set down the pretty woman at the river bank many hours ago. How come you are still carrying her along?"

This ancient Chinese Zen fable reflects the thinking of many people even today. We encounter many unpleasant things in our life. They irritate us and they make us angry. Sometimes, they cause us to be bitter or jealous. But just like the little monk, we are unwilling to let go of them. We keep carrying the excess baggage with us. We let them come back to hurt us, make us angry, make us bitter and cause us a lot of agony. Why?

It is simply because we are not willing to leave behind our excess baggage. Like the big monk, we need to set down the pretty woman and be on our way once the uncomfortable situation has passed. This will immediately free us from our anxieties and our pain over past events.

O – OPTIMISTIC ATTITUDE

Optimists can only utilise their optimum potential. They never look back. They keep heading with great hope. Life is hope and hope is life. This optimistic attitude instills the confidence and creates a die-hard attitude. An optimist never gives up.

Do Not Give Up – If You Risk Nothing, You Get Nothing

Sometimes, it is possible that the whole world will discourage you. At such times, you need to listen to yourself. Listen to your heart.

Here is a story of two frogs that fell into a deep, dry well. As they tried and jump to come out of the well, they kept falling back in. Getting out seemed impossible. In the meantime, other frogs assembled outside the well and shouted: "Stop trying. The well is too deep. You can't jump. You are destined to die. Make peace with your fate."

Listening to this, one frog stopped trying and soon, it died. The second frog kept trying. He got higher and higher with each jump and finally, he jumpes high enough to get out. The frogs outside were surprised but they cheered him. One old frog asked: "Why did you keep trying when we all shouted to tell you it was too high?"

The frog looked surprised, "Is that what you said? Actually I thought you were all shouting to encourage me to jump higher. Actually you see, I am a bit deaf!"

The moral of the story is simple: when you are in trouble, don't give up just because others say it is a no win situation.

Think for yourself. In the end, if you decide not to take the risk do so because you have investigated and analyzed all of the facts and information yourself. When you know a situation well, you will be able to grab the right opportunity, even if it comes a little later.

When you hit a rock with a hammer to break it, you might notice that nothing happens for the first many blows. But suddenly you hit it one more time. With the 100th blow, the rock breaks. Does it mean that all the 99 blows you hit previously were wasted? No, it isn't the 100, blow that knocks a strong rock down. It's the 99 that went before. Hence, you need to keep trying and never give up.

To Make or Build Optimistic Attitude Turn Scars into Stars

The great musician Beethoven was handicapped. He was deaf but he composed the best music with his optimistic attitude. John Milton was blind, he wrote the best poem on nature. Franklin D Roosevelt, the best President was handicapped. He ruled from wheel chair.

We have a lot of potential in us but we do not know how to use them. In the Ramayana, when Hanuman was asked to cross the sea and go to Lanka to see whether Sita was there, Hanuman was surprised and said to Jambavant, "How can you expect me to cross the ocean? I am only a small monkey." Jambavanth replied, "You are not merely a monkey, you are *Vayuputra* (son of wind). You have lot of energy and potential." Hanuman then realised his potential and grew big enough to cross the ocean.

Similarly, we too are unaware of our hidden potentials. *A difficult situation is just a challenge to our own hidden potentials.* We must look forward to tackling it successfully. Nothing can stop us.

Difference Between Optimistic and Pessimistic Attitude

Optimistic	Pessimistic
1. Self respect	1. Self put down
2. Self confidence	2. Self doubt
3. Self worth	3. Self abuse
4. Self acceptance	4. Self denial
5. Self love	5. Self centredness
6. Self knowledge	6. Self deceit
7. Self discipline	7. Self indulgence

Optimistic attitude means having a positive self-esteem. Self-esteem means how you feel about yourself.

Feel good factors for optimistic attitude

* Knowledge of relaxation techniques
* The ability to express your feelings

- Achievable goals to aim for
- Having time for the things you enjoy
- A healthy diet
- A sport or exercise you enjoy
- Work you find rewarding
- A comfortable balance between work and leisure
- Time yourself, to do the things in which you are interested
- Time for friends and family.

P – PROBLEM SOLVING TECHNIQUE

Problems stand for

P: Predictor of future: *It indicates the course of fortune.*

R: Responsibility to solve the problems: *It indicates that one has got the responsibility from destiny to solve the problem.*

O: Opportunity to prove self: *It gives an opportunity to prove self-skills and creativity to the world.*

B: Blessing in disguise: *It is a blessing in disguise that fetches the blessings of all well wishers.*

L: Lessons of life: *It teaches the lessons of life to be more mature.*

E: Experience for future: *It gives us experience to not only solve the problem but also to guide others to tackle it tactfully.*

M: Message of God: *It carries the message, "Best Wishes For Success" from God because we get stressed by seeing the problems in "Present", but God foresees our future and bestows us with the responsibility to solve the problem. It is God's trust in us that enables us to handle the problem successfully. It is a challenge to use our hidden potentials.*

S: Solution is there: *This indicates every problem has an inbuilt solution. We have to click the right point to solve it. Don't try to solve many problems at a time. Arrange all your problems in the form of compartments. Open only one compartment at a time only when you are free from more productive work. Let all other compartments be closed.*

In spite of putting in all efforts if you cannot change a situation don't feel unhappy and depressed about it. Remember that time is the best healer.

Analyse the Problem First

Reflect on the following story–

A king wished to select a good Chief Minister for his kingdom. In his court were four men with equal qualification to hold the post of the Chief Minister. He therefore decided to conduct a test to select one from amongst them for the post.

One day, he called all the four of them and said, "I have a lock. It is a scientific lock, made according to mathematical calculations. Tomorrow morning all of you will be given a chance to open this lock. The person who succeeds in opening this lock within the shortest time will become the Chief Minister of this kingdom."

With a desire to become the Chief Minister the men sat up the whole night, browsing ancient writings regarding locks, mathematical designing etc. and made notes. Only one amongst them looked at a few palm leaves and then went to bed.

The next day, in the king's court, the mathematical lock was brought and placed in front of the four men. The king was also present. The gigantic size of the lock astonished everyone. The three men checked their writings again and again. Then they came up, one by one, and looked at the lock. Then they started referring to their notes about the locks and tried to open the lock. The one who had gone to sleep early was the last one to come. He just came near the lock and inspected it thoroughly. To his surprise, he found the lock was not locked at all. So, without even using a key, this man opened the lock easily by removing the hook. The king appointed him as the Chief Minister. The three others in the anxiety to open the lock did not bother to check whether the lock was locked, in the first place. The fact was, the lock was not locked.

To solve a problem, one must first understand the problem. To understand the problem, the mind should be

calm, without tension or agitation. This will facilitate seeing things objectively.

How to be calm?

Just be a witness to your thoughts. Don't identify with them. See them as clouds in the sky of your awareness. Thoughts will come and go; but you don't come and go. You are just a witness. Then the mystery of calmness happens.

Is it a Problem Or an Opportunity?

A young graduate was tired of hunting for a job. After many years, he got a job of a journalist. He went to the office full of expectations and a subtle fear. The chief editor called him and said, "Today is Independence Day. A navy vessel has docked in our harbour. Navy personnel are celebrating Independence Day on that vessel. Cover this as a news item for our magazine."

First day and first assignment –

The young man ran excitedly towards the harbour. In the evening, the other reporters who went to various places like the fort, collectorate, party and so on, gathered in the main office to give finishing touches to their respective reports. The new journalist was alone, sitting soulfully, without writing anything. One of his colleagues asked him gently, "Why aren't you writing your report?"

"It is all my luck. When I try to sell flour, a high wind blows and when I go to sell salt, it rains. The very first day, my assignment has got me into trouble. The editor sent me to cover Independence Day celebrations on the navy vessel. There were no celebrations on that vessel." The young journalist expressed sardonically.

"Why?" pursued the colleague.

"There was a big hole in that vessel. People who had gathered there were busy in the preparations; hence no one noticed it. Only when a lot of water had entered the vessel, did someone notice it. Thereafter, they were busy in repairing the vessel. How on earth could they celebrate Independence Day?" asked the new journalist sulkily.

His colleague was excited. He exclaimed, "My God, that news should come on the first page." and ran out to collect further information on that mishap.

The very information that made the new journalist wilt in sorrow because he viewed it as a problem was a golden opportunity for the other to prove his talent? The new journalist had missed an opportunity, which was spotted by the other reporter.

Life is not something that happens according to a planned agenda. It is a procession of unexpected opportunities. In fact, each problem is an opportunity for us.

Reflect on the following story –

Buddha was walking through a forest. The woodcutters who were cutting wood nearby ran to him and said, "Stop, please stop. There is a terrible demon in the forest. He is a cannibal who eats human flesh. After eating a person, he cuts off the thumb and keeps it safe. In that way, he has so far collected 999 thumbs. He needs just one more to make it 1000. His plan is once the final thumb is collected – to string them all up and wear them around his neck. So, please don't go into the forest. If you go, it will be a big problem for you."

To that, Buddha replied, "I will get no better opportunity than this and entered deep into the forest.

As expected, the demon felled a huge branch of a Banyan tree and appeared in front of Buddha in a cloud of dust. But Buddha did not run away like others in fright. He stood strong and firm and said, "If killing me gives you pleasure, you may please do so. I accept the fact that you are really strong. But one thing...though you have the strength to break a branch of a Banyan tree, you can never attach it back to that tree. *It is very easy to destroy...but very difficult to join.*

"You know the art of destroying, I know the art of joining." Buddha said.

More than his words, the truth and compassion touched the demon deeply. After that, he became a disciple of Buddha. He was Anguli mal.

Let us not go into the analysis of the story. The truth of the tale is very simple. The demon was not problem for Buddha; instead it was an opportunity to protect the villagers from further misery. That is all.

Q – QUIT PETTY ATTITUDE AND REACTIVE TENDENCY

Some people quarrel over petty things. This attitude and action is detrimental to self as well as others. It creates tense atmosphere all around. So it is advisable to quit the attitude that increases the magnitude of stress. Bad habits are also one of the reasons of stress and strain. One has to get rid of bad habits to live a stress free life.

Open the Window of Wisdom to Quit Petty Attitude

A farmer once came to a Sufi saint with a problem. He said, "My wife is rearing a lot of cattle and fowl. The whole house is stinking with their odour. I am unable to even breathe. You must show me a way to escape from this nuisance."

The saint said, "Why don't you open the windows? The fresh air will drive out the odour." The farmer exclaimed, "Oh no! Then my pigeons will fly out of the house."

Very often, we behave like the farmer when it comes to the tensions that we confront. In order to protect something insignificant like the pigeons, we fail to open the window of wisdom. The result is tension and suffocation. **So, let us open wide, the windows of wisdom.**

Don't Bother for Petty Things to Remain Happy and Stress Free

(a) A young woman was playing with her child on the beach. Suddenly a huge wave dragged the child into the sea. The woman began to wail, "My baby! My baby is gone". The God of the seas heard her cry, relented and returned the child alive to the shore. The woman was overjoyed and hugged her child and showered kisses on its cheeks.

Then glancing at its feet, she noticed that one of the sandals was missing. At once, her joy was shattered and she began to wail again for the missing sandal. "Oh! one sandal is gone." **This is how we miss seeing the bigger gifts of life; we are lost in petty things.**

(b) A farmer had a bumper crop of tomatoes in one season. Yet, the farmer seemed to be very worried. His neighbours inquired of him the reason for his worry. He replied, "Normally I feed my pigs with tomatoes." The neighbours inquired, "What is the problem? You have a bumper crop this time." To this the farmer replied, "Yes I have a bumper crop but I do not have a single rotten tomato to offer to my pigs. What will I feed them with?"

To put it simply, ***happiness is like a lock and intelligence is like a key.*** *If you turn the key of intelligence in the opposite direction, it would lockup happiness.* ***If you turn it in the right direction, the doors of happiness will open.***

Develop a Pleasing Attitude

There was an arid open space. Under a scorching sun, work for constructing a temple for Lord Krishna was progressing. Workers were carrying loads of bricks on their head. A sage who happened to come along asked one of them, *"What are you doing?"* The worker screamed, *"Can you not see? I am carrying bricks."*

The sage asked the same question to another. He said smilingly, *"I am earning a living for my family."*

The sage asked yet another and he replied devotionally, *"I am performing a very sacred task of building a temple for my God."*

As we can see, through the actions are the same, attitudes are different. All of us may not be so lucky as to get the job of building a temple, but whatever tasks we perform if we do that with total involvement like that of building a temple, that itself is the best prayer. God gives us what we need more than what we want.

Discard the Crab Mentality

What is crab mentality? Do you know how crabs are caught? To catch crab a box is used of which one part is open so that the crab may enter inside. The box does not have a cover. When the box is full with crabs, it is covered. The crabs can easily come out from the box but their mentality stops them. As soon as one crab tries to come out from the box, another crab just pulls him down. Now you can think, what happens to the crab?

Similarly the leg pulling attitude in our society is the symbol of crab mentality. We must discard it. It stops our progress further.

Life is 10% What Actually Happens to Us, But 90% How We React to It

We really have no control over the 10% that consists of what happens to us. Our car may break down. The bus or train we were supposed to take may arrive late, throwing our day's schedule out of gear. We may be stuck in an unexpected traffic jam and miss an important meeting. We have no control over all this, but this forms only a tiny percentage of our life. **The other 90% is something we can control by our action and reaction to the circumstances surrounding us.**

Here is an example:

Think over a situation - You are taking breakfast with your family. Your daughter knocks over a cup of coffee onto your suit. You have no control over what just happened. What happens next will be determined by how you react.

You can scold your daughter for knocking the coffee cup over and she may break down in tears. After scolding her, you can turn to your spouse and criticise her for placing the cup too close and then go upstairs and change your shirt. Back downstairs you find that your daughter has been crying to finish the breakfast and get ready for school, so she misses the bus. Your spouse must leave immediately for work. You rush to the car and drive your daughter to school. Because you are late, you drive 40 km per hour in a 30 km per hour zone. The traffic cop at the crossing sees this and fines you. You reach late for an important meeting and to make matters worse, you have left your office cabinet keys at home. You have a miserable day at work but are not sure why everything seems to be going wrong. You look forward to going home. When you arrive home you find a small wedge in your relationship with your spouse and daughter. Why? Trace it back…all the way to that spilt coffee. Think carefully:

    a)   Did the coffee cause it?
    b)   Did your daughter cause it?
    c)   Did your colleagues cause it?

d) Did you cause it?

The answer is – 'd'. You caused it. It was not the spilt coffee, but your reaction to it that in turn, set off a chain of events that could have been avoided altogether if you had not reacted the way you did. You had no control over what happened with the coffee but you could have controlled your reaction to it.

Now consider this scenario - The coffee falls all over you. Your daughter gets terrified and is about to cry. You gently say, "It's okay my dear. Please be more careful next time." You grab a towel and rush upstairs to change. You come back down in time to look through the window and see your child getting on the bus. She turns and waves. You and your spouse kiss before you both go to work. You arrive five minutes early and cheerfully greet the staff. Your boss comments on how good a day you seem to be having.

So you see how the same incident can spiral into uncontrolled misery or it can be controlled and reined in by a mature reaction. **That's what we need to concentrate on our reaction to what happens around us.**

Here are some ways to gain control of the full 90%.

If someone says something negative about you, do not be a sponge and absorb it. Let the attack roll off like water on the glass. You don't have to let the negative comment affect you! React properly and it will not ruin your day. A wrong reaction could result in losing a friend, being fired, getting stressed out etc.

How do you react if someone cuts you off in traffic? Do you lose your temper? Pound the steering wheel? Does your blood pressure skyrocket? Do you try and bump them? Who cares if you arrive ten seconds late at work? But if you let the other driver affect you, your whole day could be ruined.

Imagine your train is late. It is going to affect your schedule for the day. Why take out your frustration on the TTE? He has no control over what is going on. Use your time to study, get to know the other passengers, etc. Why get stressed out? What will happen can be handled later too.

You now know the simple 90-10 secret. Apply it and you will be amazed at the results!

R – RAJYOGA MEDITATION

What is *Rajyoga* Meditation?

Yoga is a Sanskrit word, which literally means "link" or "union", (Just as its antonym-*vi yoga* which means "separation"). *The word Raja (or RAJ) means "King", Sovereign, or "Supreme". Thus Rajyoga is quite simply the communion of the soul (the king of its mind, intellect and all memories records of habits, tastes, latencies, instincts etc known as SANSKARA) with the supreme soul (God).*

The process of self-transformation begins through Rajyoga, which encompasses the three faculties of the soul – mind, intellect and *sanskars*. Rajyoga empowers the intellect to exercise the power of discrimination, to choose positive thoughts. Rajyoga in a broad sense is a way of life wherein spiritual knowledge *(Gyan)*, meditation *(yoga)*, inculcation of virtues *(Dharana)* and service *(Seva)* are the four pillars that sustain the yogic life. In Rajyoga meditation we use our most natural endowment of thinking to come to the realization.

In the course of practice of Rajyoga, one tunes the mind to that very subtle frequency (Alpha and Delta) on which God is radiating his love, light and might by considering the self, a soul and then by focusing a gentle stream of positive thoughts towards the Supreme Being.

God's own harmonious vibrations are received upon that same current, allowing the soul to experience the wealth of unlimited attributes of the Supreme. Peace, power and bliss are the inevitable fruits of this connection. The spirit is filled with happiness, which cannot be eqated with by any physical experience. Thus the soul becomes the master over his senses. *Mind, intellect and response patterns are soon tamed and transformed; the personality becomes clean and pure.* Within the soul there remains only the knowledge, full of silence of the consciousness of God.

Secular Concept of God Is One

Communion with God Father is essential, because He is the unlimited source of knowledge, peace, love, bliss, purity and power. But to truly commune with Him, we must accurately know

Him. This means, at the least, we must comprehend **His form, His abode and His attributes.**

The form of God has been spoken of universally in the same terms. **He is incorporeal and He is light.** *Christ, Moses, Guru Nanak and the teachers from every religion agree to this.* Sometimes, God is considered clearly as a point of light (for example the Egyptian pyramid is the image of God as a point of Light radiating his imperishable illumination downwards upon the earth. This is why, the Pharaoh wished to bask in that light at death, and built such lavish and time defying memorials.)

Views of all religions about the form of God are same

The Universal Light

All religions have portrayed the Aura, which surrounds Him, an oval or flame shaped image. The Hindus, for example worship **Shiva in the form of an oval stone,** *which represents that Supreme Flame.* **This same shape went westward with Abraham,** *who established such a symbol for worship in Mecca, and even today it is the holiest shrine of Islam, and a required object of pilgrimage in the life of a Muslim. Likewise, in the* **Jewish synagogue** *we can see the same* **holy flame, called the Nur Tamid,** *or Eternal Light, raised above the Ark of the law.*

*That form also went eastward, becoming **the Buddhist stupa**, then **evolving in China into the Pagoda**, and appeasing in **Japan**, once more as a small oval shaped stone, which certain Buddhist sects worship as **"The Peace Giver"**. Even modern offshoots of the main religions maintain the old form, though the meaning has been lost. The **Mormons in America**, for example, hold a special regard for beehives, which are of the same shape, and one can readily interpret the metaphor of God as that **Honey Hive** and His children as the bees.*

We have determined the universal belief in God as being a point of light, though without a human form. Not being physical, he takes up no space. The Supreme has then, the amazing form of an infinitesimal point of light, from which light emanates in an oval aura, just as with a candle, light emerges from a point source and assumes an oval form.

Faith in God–A Dialogue with an Atheist Professor

An atheist professor of philosophy speaks to his class on the problem, science has with God, the Almighty. He asks one of his new Christian students to stand up.

Professor: You are Christian, are you not, son?

Student: Yes, sir.

Professor: So you believe in god?

Student: Absolutely, sir.

Professor: Is God good?

Student: Sure.

Professor: Is God all-powerful?

Student: Yes.

Professor: My brother died of cancer even though he prayed to God to heal him. Most of us would attempt to help others who are ill. But God didn't. How is this God good then?

(The student stays silent.)

Professor: You can't answer, can you? Let's start again, young fellow. Is God good?

Student: Yes.

Professor: Is Satan good?

Student: No.

Professor: Where does Satan come from?

Student: From God.

Professor: That's right. Tell me son, is there evil in this world?

Student: Yes.

Professor: Evil is everywhere, isn't it? And God did make everything. Correct?

Student: Yes.

Professor: So who created evil?

(The student does not answer)

Professor: Is there sickness? Mortality? Hatred? Ugliness? All these terrible things exist in this world, don't they?

Student: Yes, sir.

Professor: So, who created them?

(The student has no answer)

Professor: Science says you have five senses that you use to identify and observe the world around you. Tell me, son.... have you ever seen God?

Student: No, sir.

Professor: Tell us if you have ever heard your God?

Student: No, sir.

Professor: Have you ever felt your God, tasted your God, smelt your God? Have you ever had any sensory perception of God for that matter?

Student: No sir, I am afraid I have not.

Professor: Yet you still believe in him?

Student: Yes.

Professor: According to empirical, testable, demonstrable protocol, science says your God doesn't exist. What do you say to that, son?

Student: Nothing, I only have my faith.

Professor: Yes. Faith. And that is the problem science has.

Student: Professor, is there such a thing as heat?

Professor: Yes.

Student: And is there such a thing as cold?

Professor: Yes.

Student: No, sir. There isn't.

(The lecture hall becomes very quiet with this turn of events.)

Student: Sir, you can have lots of heat, even more heat, superheat, mega heat, a little heat or no heat. But we don't have anything called cold. We can measure heat 458 degrees below zero, which is no heat, but we can't go any further after that. There is no such thing as cold. Cold is only a word we use to describe the absence of heat. We cannot measure cold. Heat is energy. Cold is not the opposite of heat, sir, just the absence of it.

(There is pin-drop silence in the lecture hall.)

Student: What about darkness, Professor? Is there such a thing as darkness?

Professor: Yes. What is night if there isn't darkness?

Student: You are wrong again, Sir. Darkness is the absence of something. You can have low light, normal light, bright light, flashing light... but if you have no light constantly, you have nothing and it's called darkness, isn't it? In reality, darkness isn't. If it were you would be able to make darkness darker, wouldn't you?

Professor: So what is the point you are making, young man?

Student: Sir, my point is that your philosophical premises flawed.

Professor: Flawed? Can you explain how?

Student: Sir, you are working on the premise of duality. You argue there is life and then there is death, a good God and a bad God. You are viewing the concept of God as something finite, something we can measure. Sir, science can't even explain a thought. It uses electricity and magnetism, but has never seen, much less fully understood either one. To view death as the opposite of life is to be ignorant of the fact that death cannot exist as a substantive thing. Death is not the opposite of life: just the absence of it.

Now tell me, Professor. Do you teach your students that they evolved from a monkey?

Professor: If you are referring to the natural evolutionary process, yes, of course, I do.

Student: Have you ever observed evolution with your own eyes, Sir?

(The professor shakes his head with a smile, beginning to realise where the argument is going.)

Student: Since no one has ever observed the process of evolution at work and cannot even prove that this process is an ongoing endeavor, are you not teaching your opinion, Sir? Are you not a scientist but a preacher?

(The class is in uproar.)

Student: Is there anyone in the class who has ever seen the professor's brain?

(The class breaks out into laughter.)

Student: Is there anyone here who has ever heard the professor's brain, felt it, touched or smelt it? No one appears to have done so. So, according to the established rules of empirical, stable, demonstrable protocol, science says that you have no brain, Sir. With all due respect, how do we then trust your lectures, Sir?

(The room is silent. The professor stares at the student, his face unfathomable.)

Professor: I guess you will have to take them on faith, son.

Student: That is it sir. The link between man and God is faith. That is all that keeps things moving and alive.

Brain, Mind, Consciousness and God - Beyond Modern Science: The relation between brain, mind and consciousness is a complex phenomenon, which is beyond the scope of modern science. Since, science is basically concerned with the physical universe, it deals with the material world and not the spiritual. Hence, modern science is not capable of explaining the truths of life and God beyond matter. There is the tendency to reject whatever cannot be understood through materialistic reasoning and logic. Occasionally, what cannot be explained in normal life is also attributed to God, the Supreme.

There are two channels for the acquisition of knowledge. One is the five senses. Knowledge is limited in range and is gross in content. As long as human beings are alive and continues to remain world-oriented, one can only experience transient happiness. Our association with the world is because of physical body and human mind remains steeped in love of sensuous pleasures and completely ignores the purpose of our incarnation. It is high time now for our dormant mind awakens.

What is perceptible through the five senses is incomplete. The other channel through which the awakening of the subconscious mind takes place lies beneath the normal mental awareness. Logic and normal reasoning do not bind it. By activating the subconscious mind the truths of life and knowledge of supreme can be perceived. What is difficult to understand through the normal mind can be understood through the intuitive mind.

Albert Einstein too had admitted that his theory of relativity was gained with the help of intuitive mind.

Rational knowledge is limited to the five senses while intuitive knowledge goes beyond the senses and science. The vast reservoir of rational knowledge possessed by the most learned persons today fails to explain the truth of life, existence of God and the solutions to life's problems.

Prepare from exercises to ....

Now do the following *visualisation exercise to tune your intellect.*

First visualise all Colours. See the red flag, red light, oranges, orange coloured clothes, yellow flowers of mustard, yellow clothes, green nature, green light, sky blue shirts, indigo powder and violet colour.

Now visualise yourself walking near the sea shore. See the ocean, listen to the sounds of waves, see the sands, feel that you are really over there. See the blue sky, see the union of water and the blue sky, feel the rays of peace in the sky blue colour, feel the deep peace, feel completely relaxed. Now fly in the sky and travel back into your body, radiate peace into your whole body, feel you are a peaceful soul, smile, and radiate peace all around. Chant OM five times. *Om Shanti.*

Now Contemplate and Visualise the Follwing:
Visualise yourself as a bright star and the God as the

brightest star and try to see the colour of the primary virtues with deep feeling and then meditate as follow:

Exercise-I

See yourself as a point of light as a shining star between the forehead. Feel the light of your soul is spreading into the whole face. See the light is further expanding into your whole body through neck, chest, stomach, arms, lower abdomen and both legs. See the inner body is bright inside and covered by skin from outside. Feel the focus of light into the whole body and try to see all your organs inside. Now feel that there is a red shower from the overhead source of divine light, which is entering into your whole body through crown chakra, face, neck, chest, stomach, arms, lower abdomen and both legs. Feel that you are completely relaxed. All cells and tissues are charged with divine powers. You have become disease free, energetic and ready to take on the day with courage and smile. Open your eyes and radiate powerful rays of light through your eyes all around.

Exercise-II

Outer and Inner Journey: *See a beautiful garden with varieties of flowers. Feel the cool morning breeze, see the rising sun, feel the red light falling on your body. Visualize the scene vividly with your third eye. Now see the movement of the sun from East to West. See that you are under a cool shade and the sun is bright. See the further movements of sun. Now feel the calm evening breeze, see the sunset the same red ball as sunrise. See the dusk, spot the bright star in the sky, concentrate on the star, feel the similar star between your forehead, feel that it is your soul, the spirit sitting and controlling the whole body system. Now see the showers of God's blessings in the form of violet rays of light, feel the showers giving you absolute peace. Now see the bliss entering into your body, see your face illuminated and rays are passing through neck, chest, arms, stomach, waist and finally into full legs. See the complete transparent body full of light inside, feel you are relaxed, all cells and tissues are charged, all* *abnormalities gone. Take in a deep breath and exhale it with the feeling of removing all waste from your body. Feel complete peace and joy. Do the humming exercise and OM chanting. Radiate peace and joy with smile on your face*

Exercise-III

I am the soul with the faculties of mind, intellect and sanskars. I am sitting between forehead. I am just like a shining bright star. From the AGYA CHAKRA I am controlling and directing all my sense and motor organs of my body. With the super luminal speed of a thought, I can detach myself from the cage of the body and can fly to any where in the universe and I can experience my original state and the true nature. Through the practice of soul – consciousness and meditation I can remain strong and contented internally. Come what may, I, the soul can fly to my eternal home and experience my own original attributes at any time, wherever I am, inside the room or on the road; at home or at work; in the city or in the country side, because I am the child of Almighty God and hence a master of an almighty soul. God gives me knowledge of truth and wisdom as the Supreme teacher. He has enlightened me. Thus I am an enlightened soul. God gives me peace, love and happiness as supreme Parents. Hence, I am a perfect and lovely child of God. I am the most contented soul on this earth. God has blessed me with purity, bliss, and all spiritual powers and divine virtues as supreme preceptor (Sad guru). Hence, I am a pure and innocent disciple of God. I am master almighty and a blissful soul.

Methodology of Rajyoga
(Methods or Steps to be Followed for Practicing Rajyoga)

To begin the practice of easy Rajyoga, one need not sit in any special posture. In fact, difficult postures should be avoided in favour of one's usual, easy and natural way of sitting. One may sit on the floor, use a cushion or sit comfortably on a chair. The main aim is to go beyond physical awareness of any pain, which can pull you back into the body and is counterproductive. On the other hand, if one meditates in a too comfortable position, (like lying in bed) one is prone to fall asleep. So take your own balanced approach for position.

While meditating, there is no need to close the eyes. Actually, it is better not to because the scenes created by visualization when the eyes are closed are far more distracting. Attention diminishes rapidly with closed eyes, and soon the mind starts wandering. In fact while day dreaming no one closes his eyes. Similarly, it is not day dreaming but creative visualization, which empowers us. Now follow the following methods for practicing Rajyoga in six stages:

1. Internalise Yourself: This is the first stage in which you turn yourself from mundane thoughts. Now start observing your own pattern of thoughts. This will naturally reduce the speed of your mental thoughts and then help to internalise and introspect yourself.

2. Channelise your thoughts: After internalising and introspection you organize positive thoughts and channelize them. Give them a just direction. As the flood is harmful in the same way flood of thought too is harmful. When we channelise the flooded water or store it by building dams, the same flooded water becomes the source of energy generation and irrigation. In the same way, when we channelise our positive thought pattern we get energized with positive energy.

3. Visualise the positive, pure and elevated thoughts: Simply creating positive thoughts is not going to give us relaxation. It has to be visualised by intellect (the third eye) in which the right part of our brain gets activated and creative ideas in visual forms start coming from the core of our unconscious. These positive and valuable impressions not only give relaxation to our mind and body but empower us also.

4. Divinise the visualisation process: Divinisation means connecting real self to the Supreme, the source of all powers and virtues. Visualise yourself sitting in front of the Supreme God who is your parent, teacher, and *Sadguru*. See him clearly, talk to him and receive positive vibrations of all powers from Him.

5. Realise the Divine visualisation: Now realise and feel the divine meeting a real one and start experiencing an extra ordinary sense of peace and well being. The mind plunges into more and more deeper experiences to become saturated with the living qualities of the Supreme. The soul realises itself as a point of divine illumination filled with love and might. All negativity is washed away at this stage. There is only the silence of the blissful presence of the Supreme.

6. Eternalise the realisation of divine feeling: Now eternalise the feeling or experience obtained during the fifth stage. Feel that it is eternal and cannot be forgotten. Let it become a part of our consciousness forever, which gives constant feeling of divine energy with self. Feel being ever guided by the Supreme directions. Feel being below the eternal fountain of love, joy and happiness and bliss forever. Enjoy this feeling at each step of life. At this final stage the soul becomes deeply merged in the feeling of divine intoxication forever, and this is the essence of life.

Rajyoga Exercise: Now practice the meditation in *six stages* by thinking deeply over the following thoughts. *Sit in a natural and an easy manner. Read the following words slowly, thinking and visualizing deeply over the thoughts, which they contain:*

"I withdraw my awareness from my physical organs. I become aware of my inner self – a point of light, the eternal soul. I now feel light, as the burden of physical thought diminishes. A non-material light glows in the centre of my forehead. I am the driver and my body is the car.

As my thoughts concentrate, I become light and floating. I find deep peace within and I am filled with power. I tune my mind to a new dimension, my original home, the soul world, the land of peace and silence and the land of tranquil light. I bathe in this glow, and once again I am filled up with total peace and purity. My home has no limits. I fly in this expanse of light, so free of tension. I enjoy the sweet stillness high in my home, now I am so free and light. Here in my true home – the soul world – there is another brilliant point of light... the Almighty Father is an ocean of peace, purity and power. As I come closer to this brilliant light, I become still more peaceful and light. Going deeper into this silence, I feel still and begin to explore this depth of peace. God, my sweetest friend provides me with the ecstasy of unlimited warmth and love. Gentle waves of light from this sweet ocean passing over me like a golden glow of tender love. I become so still, I feel that I have gone to the very bottom of this ocean of serenity. I taste the very essence of real peace. Peace becomes my true nature once again.

Now slowly I become aware of the physical costume – the body, yet from within I am completely peaceful and relaxed. I will maintain this awareness even during activities. I will remain detached and light while at work. Nothing can disturb me any more."

S – SELF-TRANSFORMATION BY SELF-MOTIVATION

Self-transformation leads to world transformation. Self is the lowest unit and center for holistic change. We cannot make our transformation conditional. " I have to change first" irrespective of the fact that anyone changes or not. Have a positive attitude towards day-to-day events. By changing your attitudes you can transform pain into pleasure, sorrow into happiness and criticism into blessings. *Therefore, do not transfer your tension but transform them.* Sometimes people transfer their stress to others instead of transforming self-attitude and perception.

Here is a real self-story:

Once there was a tenant. He used to pay the rent to his landlord on the first of every month after getting his salary. Once he did not got his salary and he became tense. He did not get sleep that night. His wife saw him walking about in tension at night. She asked him the reason behind the tension. Knowing that he had not got his salary, she went to the owner's house, rang the bell at night itself. The owner got up and opened the door. She just told the owner that her husband would not be able to pay the rent of that month the next day. After telling this she came back and told her husband to relax and sleep. Now the owner became tense and started walking in tension and did not sleep the whole night. Thus the tenant transfered the stress to the owner.

Motivate yourself

There are certain aspects in life on which you have control and there are others on which you do not have control. But you have to live wisely and keep motivating your self for self-transformation. Wise living includes both the controllable and un-controllable variables of life. Suppose the fact is that you come from an unhappy home, then you have no choice about that but you have a choice not to be a victim of an unhappy home by self-motivation. Reflect on the following story:

A father and his two sons lived in a single room. The father used to come home drunk every day and watch TV disturbing his children's studies. The eldest son was committed and concentrated on his studies, while the younger son followed the footsteps of his father. Both the children grew up. The eldest son got an award for being the best citizen in the town while on the same day; the younger son was imprisoned for a heinous crime.

When both were interviewed, the answers they gave were worth pondering. The younger son said, "All because of my father, who created a bad atmosphere at home I have become a criminal." The eldest son said, "I attribute my success to my drunken father and the unhappy home atmosphere. It was an inspiration for me that motivated me to be different."

The situation was the same but the response was different. More than the situation it is how we respond to the situation for self-motivation that determines the quality of our life.

Develop Self-confidence to Motivate and Transform Self

Research done on successful people reveals that **self-confidence is the most important factor in life for self-motivation to transform self.** It can be easily understood by the stool model.

Just imagine a stool with four legs. If one of the legs is weak, the stool is weak. The four legs represent self-confidence, which has components such as –

- Feeling Good
- Taking responsibility
- Being accountable
- Developing skills

Feeling good involves, being authentic and not pretending. Our life is a struggle involving pretensions of what we are not and in the process we do not feel good.

Reflect on this

A manager appeared to be busy on his phone and computer at the same time. Two persons sitting in front of him were vying for his attention. The manager pretended to be busy and did not have the time to even greet them. After a while, he sought the reasons for their coming. One of them said that he had come to repair his telephone, while the other said that he had come to repair his computer.

Why do we pretend? A pretending self creates false images in us, which ultimately lowers our self-esteem. Self-esteem will improve if the pretending self is dropped.

Responsible children possess good leadership qualities. It is the duty of parents to inculcate responsibility in their children and make them accountable. Such responsibility motivates them to develop new skills. This in turn builds self-confidence in them.

A research conducted on various successful people proved a fact – their success was not because of knowledge or family background, but because of their ability to see gaps in any given opportunity; just the way a creeper passes through plants and creates its own path for growth.

The ability to see gaps or potential and work on those gaps is the real skill in successful living. For example, even a concrete bridge, if constantly struck by a sparrow at a particular spot sufficient number of times may collapse. This is a well known law in Physics. So too, there are right gaps in any given situation.

Successful people adopt the right strategy at the right time in any given situation. Even in competition they do not create conflicts, but harmony. Successful people are able to see potential gaps in any particular business. Seeing these gaps and encashing on them, is a great skill. This is the secret behind successful people's strategy. For example, in a table, a common man cannot see gaps, but protons, neutrons, electrons are in motion. The table is an energy centre and not a sheer matter. There are gaps, which only scientists can see.

Consider your critics as your well-wishers.

By describing your weaknesses and drawbacks they are acting as a psychotherapist without taking any fees. **Reflect on the following story:**

Once *Buddha was walking with his disciples. A group of villagers came to Buddha and reprimanded him, as a lot many youngsters had become his disciple. After patiently listening to them he said, "My disciples in the next village are awaiting my discourse, so please allow me to go. On my return you can present whatever complaints you have against me. These words were uttered peacefully and with kindness.*

The villagers were shocked and asked, "Are you not upset by our harsh words? You listen to our accusations as though we are complimenting you."

Buddha answered their question with a question, "As a monk I am not supposed to take food twice on any day. Suppose you are not aware of this and after treating me to lunch, you also prepare dinner for me. You look forward to my company at dinner and I don't come. Would your food go waste?"

The villagers replied. "No, we would distribute the meal prepared, amongst ourselves."

"In the same way, Buddha continued his reply, the criticism you heaped on me, as I would not be carrying, it would remain with all of you. Hence I am not hurt."

Along with his disciples, Buddha continued on his way silently. On the way he told his disciples "I am feeling very hot." The disciples were shocked since it was a very cold day. He continued, "I am not talking of the external heat. I see in your minds there is seething anger at the way the villagers behaved. Instead of being compassionate you are all upset and it is that heat that I am sensing now."

There are two types of actions;
- The actions of our body
- The actions of our thoughts and feelings.

What impacts the quality of our life is the movement of thoughts and feelings. More than negative experiences it is their negative interpretations that affect our life to a great degree and self-transformation becomes difficult.

T – THINK POSITIVE

Think Positive and Make a Difference in Others' Lives

A man was walking on the sea beach in the morning. He saw that hundreds of starfish were coming with the waves and when the waves went back, the starfish die due to heat of the sun. As long as waves were there the starfish were alive. The man advanced some steps. He picked up a fish and threw it in the water. He kept on doing that. A man was right behind him and he could not understand what this man was doing. He came near him and asked, "What are you doing? Hundreds of fish are here, how many will you save them all? And does it make any difference?" The man did not reply, he went two steps ahead to pick up a fish and threw it into the water and said, "Due to this act, one of the fish got affected."

A True story:

A teacher in New York decided to honour each of her final year students in high school by telling them the difference each of them made to her life. She called each student to the front of the class, one at a time. First she told each of them how they had made a difference to her and the class.

Then she presented each of them with a blue ribbon imprinted with gold letters, which read, "Who I am makes a difference."

Afterwards the teacher decided to do a class project to see what kind of impact the recognition had on the community. She gave each of the students three more ribbons and instructed them to go out and spread this acknowledgment ceremony. Then they were to follow up on the results, see who honoured whom and report back to the class in about a week.

One of the boys in the class went to a junior executive in a nearby company and honoured him for helping him with his career planning. He gave him a blue ribbon and put it on his shirt. Then he gave him two extra ribbons and said, "We are doing a class project on recognition, and we would like you to go out find somebody to honour, give him a blue ribbon, then give him the extra blue ribbon so that he too can acknowledge a third person to keep this acknowledgment ceremony going. Then please report back to me and tell me what happened."

Later, that day the junior executive went in to see his boss, who had been known, by the way, as being kind of a grouchy fellow. He sat his boss down and he told him that he deeply admired him for being a creative genius. The boss seemed very surprised. The junior executive asked him if he would accept the gift of the blue ribbon and give him permission to put it on him. His surprised boss said, "Well, sure." The junior executive took the blue ribbon and placed it right on his boss's jacket above his heart.

As he gave him the last extra ribbon, he said, "Would you do me a favour? Would you take this extra ribbon and pass it on by honouring somebody else? The young boy who first gave me the ribbons is doing a project in school and we want to keep this recognition ceremony going and find out how it affects people."

That night the boss came home to his 14 years. old son and sat him down. He said, "The most incredible thing happened to me today. I was in my office and one of the junior executives came in, admired me and gave me a blue ribbon for being a creative genius. Imagine, he thinks, I am a creative genius. Then he put one of his blue ribbon that says, 'Who I am makes a difference,' on my jacket above my heart. He gave me an extra ribbon and asked me to find somebody else to honour. As I was driving home tonight, I started thinking about whom I should honour with this ribbon and I thought about you. I want to honour you, my days are really hectic and when I come home I don't pay a lot of attention to you. "Sometimes, I scream at you for not getting good grades in school and for your bedroom being a mess, but somehow tonight, I just wanted to sit here and, well, just let you know that you do make a difference to me. Besides your mother, you are the most important person in my life. You are a great kid and I love you."

The startled boy started to sob and he couldn't stop crying. His whole body shook. He looked up at his father and said through his tears, 'Dad, earlier tonight I sat in my room and wrote a letter to you and Mom explaining why I had killed myself and asking you to forgive me. I was going to commit suicide tonight after you were asleep. I just didn't think that you cared at all. The letter is upstairs. I don't think I need it after all."

His father walked upstairs and found a heartfelt letter full of anguish and pain. The envelope was addressed, "Mom and Dad."

The boss went back to work as a changed man. He was no longer a grouch but made sure to let all his employees know that they made a difference. The junior executive helped several other young people with career planning and never forgot to let them know that they made a difference in his life...one being the boss's son.

And the young boy and his classmates learned a valuable lesson. Who you are DOES make a difference.

You never know what kind of difference a little encouragement or just a smile can make to a person. Know that someone thinks that you are important, or you wouldn't have received the encouragement in the first place. Remember that! I gave you a blue ribbon. **Who you are makes a difference and I want you to know that.**

It is nice to be important.

But it is more important to be nice.

How Positive Thinking Helps to Recover From Diseases

*When the celebrated French cyclist, Lance Armstrong, was diagnosed with **testicular cancer with a 40 percent survival chance** and told that he'd never be able to cycle again, his first thought was, "I am going to die". On second thoughts, he decided to fight back and declared himself a cancer survivor instead of being a cancer victim. Later, when he coughed up blood, he told himself there was nothing to worry as he'd coughed up only "a little blood". A few years later, not only was Lance declared cancer free, he even won the Tour de France cycling championship, again.*

While the doctors found his recovery unbelievable, Lance firmly believed that a *mind that thinks positive could conquer the body.* There is a similar example of positive thinking back home.

Himadri Paul, a student of IIT, Mumbai, was sitting on a second floor balcony railing one day, when he lost his balance and went hurtling down to hit the concrete below. He suffered *multiple fractures in his spinal cord, broke both legs and one hand.* Doctors provided no guarantee that he'd ever walk again. Devasted, Himadri began looking for hope in the Bhagwad Gita. The Gita says, "You must overcome your weakness to make progress." He realised that thinking that he couldn't ever walk again was his weakness. So he decided to believe in his recovery. He took his first step after one-and-a-half years. Today, he is back at IIT. Thanks to positive thinking once again.

However, how much scientific proof does positive thinking really have? *Lab tests have proved that there is a lower count of white blood cells, which fight infections, among depressed people.* Thus, our moods do have a bearing on our immunity function. Clinical studies also show that stress can impede wounds from healing, and impair the effectiveness of vaccines.

In August 2002, results of a study conducted at the Yale University in US were published, which showed that *optimists lived seven years longer than pessimists.* The study used 660 subjects, who were asked questions that revealed their outlook. Researchers then followed the fate of these 660 subjects over the next 23 years. According to this study, *positive thinking is more important in longevity than lower blood pressure and cholesterol levels.* Gloomy people have cells that age more rapidly. This difference in the rate of cellular ageing is equivalent to reducing seven years off a pessimists lives.

According to a Banglore based Dr Deepak Sharan, an orthopaedic surgeon, *"Positive thinking has been proved to affect musculoskeletal disorders."* Dr John Sarno of the New York University School of Medicine, has showed that *psychological factors often trigger back pain and other musculoskeletal disorders, instead of structural defects.* It's called *"tension myositis syndrome", where pain acts as a diversion from negative thoughts. The brain reduces blood flow to the affected areas, resulting in a build-up of waste materials and inducing pain.*

Positive thinking translates to positive vibes for babies as well. Mother's touch is essential for the survival of sick babies," says Dr Armeida Fernandez, a Mumbai based pediatrician. "Mothers must hold their babies and convey the positive message to their babies that they must live."

Focus on the Positive and Work Smart

You are to tell me what you observe about the following equations:

$3+4=7$ $9+2=11$ $8+4=13$ $6+6=12$

Tell me, what did you observe?

While conducting this test, more than 90 percent of the participants immediately say, 8+4 is not 13 but it is 12. That is true and they are correct. But they could have also observed that the three other equations were right. That 3+4 is 7, that 9+2 is 11, and that 6+6 is 12.

What is my point? *Many people immediately focus on the negative instead of the positive.* Most of us focus on what is wrong with other people rather than what is right about ourselves. Examine those four equations.

Three were right and only one was wrong. But what is the knee-jerk observation? It is the wrong equation. If 10 people you didn't know were to walk through a door, most of you would describe those people by the negative points about them such as, he is fat, he is bald etc.

It is always the negative we focus on and not the positive. You will definitely experience this in the corporate world. You do a hundred good things and make one mistake. Guess what? Chances are, your attention will be called to that one mistake.

So what's better than focusing on the negative? Believe me, its focusing on the positive. *If this world could learn to focus on the positive more than the negative, it would be a much nicer place to live in.*

What's better than working hard? We have always been told to work hard. Our parents say that our teachers say that, and our principal says that. But there is something better than merely working hard. *It is working SMART. It is taking time to understand the situation, and coming out with an effective and efficient solution to get more done with less time and effort. As the Japanese say, "there is always a better way."*

Smart mind for success:

There is a toothpaste production company in US, producing high quality toothpaste that is well received by the consumers. For the first 10 years, the sales increased by 10-20% every year. This pleased the shareholders and the management. But when they entered into the 11th, 12th and 13th years, sales became stagnant. The board of directors were very unhappy about the performance and called for a national management meeting to find a solution.

In the meeting, one young manager stood up and spoke to the board, "In my hand there is an envelope and it contains a suggestion. If you want to use my suggestion, you must agree to pay me $50000 for it."

The president got very angry on hearing this demand. "I am paying you your salary, allowances and bonus. You are also part of our profit sharing plan. Now I ask for a suggestion and you want another $50000. Don't you think this is a bit too much?"

"Mr President," replied the young man. "Please do not misunderstand my request. The salary that you pay is for working hard for the company everyday. But this is a very important and valuable suggestion and I believe you should pay extra for it. If you think that my suggestion is not worthy, you can throw it away and pay me nothing. But, if you do not look at it, what you lose will be more than $ 50000.

"Alright," said the president. "Let me see what suggestion is worth $ 50000."

So he took the envelope and read the contents. He then took a cheque leaf and signed a cheque for $50000 and gave it to the young man.

This is what was written on a piece of paper inside the envelope: "Enlarge the opening of the current tube by 1mm."

The president immediately ordered this suggestion to be implemented. Just imagine, every morning, every consumer will consume a little additional toothpaste and the total daily consumption of the product will increase, obviously manifold. Last heard, this suggestion alone increased the sales for the 14th year, by a whopping 32%, quite like the savings made by the airline by reducing one olive in the salad served in first class.

U – UNIVERSAL BROTHERHOOD AND FATHERHOOD

We are children of one God and we are all brothers. Therefore, barriers of caste, creed, regions, and religions stand demolished with this concept. *This concept unites globally for making a better world to live in peace and happiness.*

Some people think that 'spirituality' is associated with rituals, religious bigotry, blind faith and fundamentalist attitudes. Some people believe that spirituality is religion. Some people are scornful of the very reference of spirituality. They blame spirituality for all the religious fundamentalism, associated atrocities, caste rivalry, religious segregation and, meaningless traditional and customary practices.

Religions are nothing but the different choices of faith available to humankind. It is the right of an individual to adopt faith and principles in his life. There is freedom of choice. Respecting the freedom of choice is the best choice for others to directly or indirectly help peaceful coexistence.

Spirituality is universal. Spirituality goes beyond the boundary of religious practices and covers the entire humankind. Spirituality is the spiritual dimension of an individual. One is a spiritual being and not a physical being whether one accepts it or not.

Practice Humility

Many years back, a horse rider saw some soldiers who were failing to lift up a bundle of wooden log. The captain was standing there as the soldiers were struggling. The horse rider asked the captain why he did not help them. The captain replied, "I am the captain and my duty is to order them only." Then the horse rider got off from the horse and helped the soldiers to lift the wooden log, the horse rider quietly got on the horse and told the captain, "you call your commander-in-chief next time if you need any help." After the horse rider went away, the captain and soldiers came to know that the horse rider was George Washington.

V – VISUALISE YOUR SUCCESS TO REALISE IT

"Success is our birth right". Read this powerful thought daily and nurture it in your subconscious mind through visualisation process. This is the eternal source of dynamism, courage and self-motivation and reduces stress to minimum.

Use Your Power of Third Eye for Success in Life

The true inner meaning of success is to be successful in the enterprise of living. A long period of peace, joy and love on this earth may be termed as success. The eternal experience of these qualities is the everlasting success in the life. The real things of life such as peace, harmony, integrity, security and happiness are intangible. They come from the deep self of human beings. *Meditating on and visualising these qualities builds these real treasures of life in our memory bank.* *That is the true place where moth and rust do not affect and where thieves do not break through and steal.*

The four steps to success –

Step-1. Love your work: The first vital step to success is to find out the things you love to do and then do it. Unless you love your work, you cannot make it possible. Consider yourself successful at it, even if the rest of the world hails you as a great failure. By loving your work, you have a deep desire to carry it out. If you don't know your true expression, ask for guidance and it will come.

Step-2. Specialise in your work: The second step to success is to specialize in some particular field of your choice and strive to excel in it. Learn more about it than anyone else. There is an enormous contrast between this attitude of mind and that of someone who wants only to make a living just get by. "Getting by" is not true success. A person's motives must be greater, noble and more altruistic.

Step-3. Holistic attitude: The third step is the most important. You must be sure that the things you want to do, do not contribute only to your success. Your desire must not be selfish. It may benefit humanity. Your idea must go further with the purpose of blessing or serving the world. It will then come back to you magnified and full of blessings. If you work only for your benefit, you do not complete the essential circuit. You may appear to be successful but the short circuit you have generated in your life may lead to overtime the limitation or sickness.

Someone may seem to succeed for a while, but money obtained by fraud often have wings and flies away. When we rob another, we rob ourselves. The mood of lack and limitation that led to our behaviour manifests itself in other ways as well, in our body, our home life and our relationship with others. There is no success without peace of mind. What is the good if a person accumulates wealth and spend sleepless nights, is either sick or has a guilty complex.

Step-4. Visualise your success repeatedly: A successful person loves his work and expresses himself fully. Success is contingent upon a higher ideal than the mere accumulation of riches. *The person of success is the person who possesses great psychological and spiritual understanding.* Many of the great business leaders of today depend upon the correct use of their subconscious mind for their success. They cultivate the ability to visualise an upcoming project as if it were already complete. Having seen and felt the fulfillment of their affirmative prayers, their latent impressions get activated and bring about their realization. If you visualise an object clearly, you will be provided with the necessities, in ways you know not of, through the wonder working power of your memory bank.

*The latent impressions of success are the energy behind all the steps in any plan of success. Your thought must be creative. Thought fused with feeling becomes a subjective faith or belief and according to **your belief it is done unto you.***

Once you understand that you possess a mighty force within you that is capable of helping you to realise all your desires, you gain both confidence and a sense of peace. Whatever your field of action may be, you should learn the law of your memory bank. When you know how to use your power of third eye to unlock the memory bank and activate the latent impressions of success, you are on the sure path of true success. If you are about God's business, or any part of it, God by his nature is for you, so who can be against you? With this understanding there is no power in heaven or on earth that can withhold success from you.

Remember your subconscious mind is a storehouse of memory. For a perfect memory affirm frequently and repeatedly through visualisation of your third eye about your true concept of success.

W – WATCH YOUR WATCH
(Words, actions, thoughts, character and habits)

"Word" is very important. "Wound heals faster but wound of words never heals." So watch your each word. Watch your actions too because you are being watched by millions of viewers on the stage of world's eternal drama. So be a good actor. Thoughts are the root of all actions, so care for each thought. Character is the pillar of life, so make it the strongest. Habits form our character, so nurture good habits. It is rightly said –

"Sow the seeds of thoughts and reap an attitude.
Sow the seeds of attitude and reap an action
Sow the seeds of actions and reap a habit
Sow the seeds of habits and reap a character
Sow the seeds of character and reap a destiny"

Nurture a winning habit

When a young person completes his education and embarks on his career, he is like a young horse in a racecourse, full of energy, talented and enthusiastic about the future, but no one wants to invest in him. This horse wants to run and win races, wants his potential to be utilized in a more efficient manner. For that he needs an experienced jockey. In the case of a fresh graduate college, his professor, relative or a godfather can play the role of at jockey.

Then the trained horse and his experienced jockey will hunt for a gambler who will put his money on the capabilities of the horse and give them that first chance. They grab the opportunity and try to win races for the gambler. The gambler is so assured of the speed of the horse and the talent of the jockey that the initial setbacks don't bother him.

Soon, the horse tastes blood and starts winning races. *During the lifetime of the horse, the jockey may change, even the gambler may change, but the horse never gets out of its winning habit. So be a winning horse on the racecourse of your life.*

X – X-RAY YOUR INNER PERSONALITY (SELF IMAGE) DAILY

Before going to bed just check any negative spots on the X-Ray film of your inner personality (self image). *Check it and change it till negativity vanishes completely.*

Self image: The X-Ray of our personality

The self-image that we show to everyone is external and the result of our internal self-esteem. It is just like X-ray of our outer appearances. A healthy self-image is a flawless X-ray. It is associated with the feelings of competence, confidence and self-worth. It is very much essential in order to make a positive impression on others. *If you feel good about the way you look and the things you have, it is very likely that you will have high self-esteem.*

Reflect on the following: Long ago in a small, far away village, there was a house of 1000 mirrors. A small, happy little dog learnt of this place and decided to visit it. When he arrived, he bounced happily up the stairs to the doorway of the house. He looked through the doorway with his ears lifted high and his tail wagging as fast as it could. To his great surprise, he found himself staring at 1000 other happy little dogs with their tails wagging just as fast as his. He cheered up with a great smile, and was answered with 1000 great smiles just as warm and friendly. As he left the house, he thought to himself, "This is a wonderful place. I will come back and visit it often."

In this same village, another little dog, who was not quite as happy as the first one, decided to visit the house of 1000 mirrors. He slowly climbed the stairs and hung his head low as he looked into through the door. When he saw the 1000 unfriendly looking dogs staring back at him, he growled at them and was horrified to see 1000 little dogs growling back at him. As he left, he thought to himself, "That is a horrible place and I will never go back there again."

All the faces in the world are mirrors. What kind of reflections do you see in the faces of the people you meet? What reflection do others see when they look at you? Where you come from is where you will go. *The most important opinion you have is the one you have of yourself and the most significant things you say all day are things you say to yourself.*

How many people have you seen who walk around with their head bowed and back slouched? What do you think this says about their self-esteem? Do you think that they will be able to sell themselves?

Winners present a dignified presence to the world. They are confident and they walk tall. Their manner lets people know: "I am a good person. I deserve to be respected."

Losers tend to think that appearances aren't important. They want to be accepted as they are. Whether we like it or not, appearances do count a lot in today's society. But it is not what you look like that counts, it is how you feel about what you look like that affects your confidence and your self esteem.

How 'Alfred Nobel' X-rayed His Image and Changed Himself

Approximately hundred years back, a man was surprised

early in the morning when he saw his name in the obituary column in the newspaper. His name was printed by mistake. Reading this, initially he was shocked about whether he was live or dead. Later when he cooled down, he thought that he should see, what people had said about him? It was written about him, "*The king of dynamite died and he was the merchant of death.*" This man had discovered dynamite.

Having read this in the newspaper, he questioned himself, "Will I be remembered in this manner by people"? This feelings touched his heart and he decided that he never wanted to be remembered like that. Since that day, he started working for peace. His name was Alfred Nobel. Now he is associated with the world's highest peace prize-Nobel Prize.

Y – YOGASANA

Yogasana is the important technique to get rid of diseases in physical body. Besides *Rajyoga* meditation, that must be a part of daily routine to keep our body disease free and stress free. This is part of **active meditation**. This channelises the energy into the whole body. This is known as *HATH Yoga. Passive meditation is known as Rajyoga.*

The following table explains the *differences between active and passive meditation:*

Active meditation	Passive meditation
1. It activates energy centers of the physical body	1. It purifies the mental body to activate energy centers in physical body
2. It makes our body flexible	2. It makes our mind peaceful, intellectual, creative and sharpens memory

Active meditation	Passive meditation
3. It makes us tired if not integrated with the visualisation power of third eye	3. It increases the level of reserve energy (potential energy) to make us dynamic
4. It is done in empty stomach and twice in a day, preferably in the morning and evening time	4. It can be done at any time and many times in a day. Best time is *Amritbela*.
5. It co-ordinate our solar and lunar energy centers	5. It co-ordinates mental, intellectual and spiritual centers of self with the cosmic power
6. It keeps the brain active with beta activities	6. It gives relaxation to mind and brain with alpha, theta and delta activities

Z – ZEAL AND ENTHUSIASM

Every great man has his past and every ordinary man has got the future in hand to become great. No great man was born great. They became great by their patience, perseverance and glorious act. They became the real actors in their life and powered themselves as great hero on this world stage. They are "Ideal" for us.

Be A History Maker Not A History Reader

It is true: 95% of people in this world only read history. There is only a small 5% minority who makes history. The question is, which category you want to be in; the majority of history readers or the minority of history makers.

To make a history you have to have a vision. A vision can be described as seeing things (a desired future state) that are not immediately visible. A vision provides us with a purpose in life, giving it meaning and direction. A vision is a realization that leads to maturity and an understanding of our responsibility to our family, our community, our organization and our souls. When we fail to identify what is right for us, we move into the wilderness, torn by confusion.

Examine your vision by answering these questions:

1. What exactly do I want from my life? Be specific and focused.
2. Why do I want and what I want? Have clarity.
3. How would I feel after accomplishing my goals? Visualize.
4. Are my accomplishments in conformity with my core values?
5. Do I feel passionate and deeply emotional about the desired outcome? Will it be meaningful and give me values for existence?

One night, the Greek philosopher, astronomer and mathematician Thales was walking down a street. He was so engrossed in observing the stars that he fell into a ditch. An elderly women helped him out and after recognizing him, said, "Here is a person who studies the stars but cannot see what lies below his feet."

So remember, even if you are highly focused, never lose sight of the surrounding environment.

Dhirubhai Ambani once said, "Think big, think fast, and think ahead. *Ideas are no one's monopoly. Our dreams have to be bigger, our ambitions higher, our commitment deeper and our efforts greater.* This is my dream for Reliance and India. *Don't give up. Courage is my conviction."*

Old Age is a Change, Welcome It

Old age, is not a tragic occurrence. What we call the aging process is really a choice. It is to be welcomed joyfully and gladly. Each phase of human life is a step forward on a path that has no end. We have enormous powers that transcend the limit of our bodily power. We have marvellous senses that transcend the limit of our five physical senses. Life is a self-renewing process. There is nothing like old age. Our body's cells and tissues keep renewing themselves. Our physical body is barely eleven months old because our permanent memory renews it every eleven months.

Many old aged people think that no one wants them. They are of no use to anyone. They think that they were born, grew up, got old and would die and that is the end of the story. Some people are afraid of what they term as "Old age", the end and extinction.

Age is the flight of years, but the dawn of wisdom. *Wisdom is the awareness of the tremendous spiritual powers and the knowledge of how to apply these powers to lead a full and happy life.*

Old age can be the beginning of a glorious, fruitful, active and most productive life pattern, better than any, one has ever experienced.

Old age may be called the contemplation of the truths of God from the highest standpoint. The joys of old age are greater than those of youth. Nature slows your body so that you may have the opportunity to meditate on things divine. Grey hairs are an asset. **Old men do not sell their grey hairs but they sell their talent, abilities, and wisdom that they have gathered through the years.**

Retirement is a new venture to take up studies and interests. You can do the things you always wanted to do, when you were so busy making a living. Give your attention to living life, becoming a producer and not a prisoner of society in the old age. Fear of old age can bring about physical and mental deterioration. *You grow old when you cease to dream and when you lose interest in life. You grow old if you are irritable, crotchety, petulant and cankerous.*

Fill your mind with truths of God and radiate the sunshine of His love. *The Greek philosopher Socrates learnt to play musical instruments when he was eighty years old. Michel Angelo was painting his greatest canvases at eighty.*

The fruits of old age are love, joy, peace, patience,
gentleness, goodness, faith, meekness and temperance.

Learn How to be Active and Dynamic to Remain Young for Ever

Many people take fad drugs, follow fad diets and waste their money on flimsy exercise machines whose virtues are touted on television. The rich go in for spa treatments, liposuction and cosmetic surgery. Their constant and futile cry is "Look I can keep up with the best of them."

Diets, multivitamins and supports of all kinds will not keep these people young. They must realise that they grow old or remain young in accordance with their processes of thinking. Our memory is conditioned by other thoughts. If your thoughts are constantly on the beautiful, the noble and the good, you will remain spiritually young regardless of your chronological years.

You are as young as you think you are. You are as strong as you think you are. You are as useful as you think you are. You are as young as your thoughts.

Do the following third eye exercise early in the morning when you wake up:

Visualise the days of your youth. Feel the miraculous healing, self renewing power of your memory bank. See the mental movies of your active and dynamic days. Replay the past impressions in front of your third eye. Know and feel that you are inspired, lifted up, rejuvenated, revitalised and recharged spiritually. You can bubble over with enthusiasm and joy. Just like the days of your youth, for the simple reason that you can always mentally and emotionally recapture that joyous state.

Feel the focus of divine light upon your head. Feel that it is revealing you need to know. It enables you to affirm the presence of your good, regardless of appearances.

Get a vision of yourself as happy, radiant, successful, serene and powerful. Feel that the secret of youth is love, joy, inner peace and laughter. Feel that in divine light there is no darkness at all. Feel that you are a child of the infinite life that knows no end. You are an heir to eternity. You are wonderful.

Feel the zeal and enthusiasm and open your eyes to start the day with full vigour and strength.

● ● ●

12

HEALING POWER OF MIND
(MY EXPERIENCE)

Healing Through Mind

The mind is like a kite, intellect is like a thread and the *prana* (life force that is self) is like the person flying the kite. Unless the person flying the kite has his attention on the thread, the kite will fly helter-skelter. So, the *prans,* which, thought it means life force, is loosely interpreted as breath for the sake of convenience in doing PRANAYAMA.

But *Rajyoga* is an advanced practice where the practitioner heightens his awareness of the life force, using it as a form of subtle but powerful meditation. Anybody who has flown a kite knows the difference between one just holding the thread and the skilled person who can make the kite draw patterns on the sky, ride every puff of wind instead of being dragged by it. With *Rajyoga*, the person assumes this expertise with the self. It is also a powerful healing practice, used to cure both oneself and others.

Neurology proves that there are different maps in the physical brain itself. These maps keep changing through our lives. For example, the phantom limb pain (ache in the body part which has been amputated) was for long thought by scientists to be wishful thinking, a figment of imagination of the victim. Today, it is proved that though the body part is lost, the brain accommodates its map of sensitivity to some other place. May be the cheek. So every time the person winces, the brain interprets this movement of the cheeks as pain of the phantom limb.

Similar to such maps, the body has its own maps and blueprints for various systems (endocrinological map, for instance). One neurologist observes that these several blueprints road maps within the body work in a complex intertwining fashion. Though working in tandem, they are separately designed as per nature and nurture.

Power of mind is tremendous provided a powerful self guides his mind. There is no point in telling that my mind is powerful and I am weak. A spiritually weak person cannot guide his own mind to bring out the desired result. Intellect is the key, which is to be turned in the right direction by a powerful self to open the lock of subconscious /unconscious mind and activate the impression of primary virtues to heal self and also heal the body.

Condition for Healing Through Mind

1. **End your doubt, hesitation and fear:** Doubts, hesitation and fear weaken our mind. It blocks the flow of the power of mind. Don't say to yourself, "I wish I could be healed" or "I hope this works". Our feeling about the work to be done sets the tone. Harmony is ours and health is ours.

When our desires in conscious mind and visualisation by third eye are in conflict due to doubts and fear, our visualisation invariably gains the way.

Suppose you were asked to walk along one feet wide wall of two feet high. You would do it easily, without question. But now suppose the height of the same wall is raised to twenty feet, would you walk on it? You, probably would not do it. Your desire to walk would come into conflict with your visualisation. You would visualise yourself falling off along the way to the ground. You might very much want to walk across the wall but fear of falling would keep you away from being able to do it. The more effort you put into conquering your visualisation or suppressing it through your desire, the greater strength is given to the dominant visual imagery of falling. May be you find yourself thinking –

* I want a healing, why can't I get it?

* I try so hard, why don't I get result?

* I must force myself harder.

Now you can realise where the error lies for not getting healed by your own mind power.

These are all due to mental pressures. Mental pressures raise your brain's beta activities and the doors of memory bank get automatically locked. Power of mind cannot flow.

2. **Mental Purity:** Mental impurities like lust, anger, hatred, jealousy, .ego, greed etc. cloud the mind power and healing becomes impossible. Therefore, it is necessary to purify our mind by practicing *Rajyoga* and then activate the power of the mind for healing the diseases.

3. **Pure Vegetarian Diets:** Pure vegetarian diet create positive energy in our bodies where as non-vegetarian diets create negative and toxic energy in our bodies. Negative and toxic energy block the mind power and healing becomes impossible. Even the use of onion and garlic in vegetarian diets are prohibited while using mind power because its bad odour not only creates toxic energy in the body but also it deflects the cosmic energy tapped by mind power for healing the physical body.

Some people use onion and garlic as antibiotic. It is a well known fact that the excess use of antibiotic not only impairs our natural immune system but produces side effects also. It may be used for certain time period as a medicine but not advisable at all if a person practises healing through mind power. That is why, it is said that as is the food so is the mind.

4. **Select a place and fix the time:** We should select a place of serene environments full of positive energy. It may be a temple, a prayer hall or a prayer room at home, meditation centre etc. For quick result, fix a time in the morning for half an hour between 4 AM and 5 AM to practise healing through mind. Because early in the morning we remain in alpha state of mind due to the presence of abundance positive energy, cosmic energy and infrared rays in the environment.

5. Regular practise for 28 days minimum without any break : Practise healing through the mind at the same time and at the same place not only programme our memory and activate the impressions of healing but also it creates a powerful positive energy zone, where any body would feel peace of mind after coming over to that place. Breaking of from the schedule is not advisable at all if you want healing must follow. This is because it activates the impressions of memory of healing permanently to bring out complete healing. This *Rajyoga* exercise must be done with full faith and confidence regularly.

Casual exercise creates impressions for very short duration similar to a line drawn on water.

Regular exercise for 14 days creates impressions similar to the lines drawn on sand. This lasts for short duration.

Regular exercise for 28 days and more creates the impressions similar to the lines drawn on stones or on a rock. This leaves permanent impression.

A miracle will definitely happen if you adhere to the above conditions.

How I Healed Myself From Life Threatening Diseases?

When I understood the self-concept through the *Rajyoga* Meditation, I started guiding the mind through my intellect to activate the healing impressions of my memory. I never thought that I am diseased or weak. I thought myself as a driver and mechanic who would repair the vehicle of the body. I was sure that healing would follow and these medicines would definitely cure me. I also visualised myself in good health and without any diseases. I was very thankful to God for providing treatment through doctors and nursing staffs. I kept on radiating peaceful and powerful rays of God all around the hospital. I practised the following meditation exercise during chemotherapy regularly without fail and with full faith and confidence.

Photograph of B.K. Chandra Shekhar during Chemotherepy treatment of cancer.

Meditation Exercise to release power of mind:

I withdraw my awareness from my physical organs, I become aware of my inner self, a point of light... the eternal soul... I now feel light... and a non-material light glows in the centre of my forehead... and I am the driver of the body... body is like the car which has to be repaired...

As I concentrate on my thought I become light... floating... I find deep peace within... and I am filled with power... I tune my mind to a new dimension, the land of peace and silence... there is another brilliant point of light... the almighty father... who is all-powerful and blissful... I become still... I feel real peace... I see powerful rays of red colour... started falling on me and on my body... and starts healing the cancerous cells and tissues... I focused the rays just like a welder does on the diseased part or organ and feels like burning the cancerous cells... I feel complete healing, my cells and tissues are rejuvenated... Almighty father empowered me... I am a powerful soul... I radiate powers all around through my eyes... *Om Shanti, Om Shanti, Om Shanti.*

•••

13

HEALTHY LIVING

Holistic Health

Holistic Health means Whole Health, which includes a good health from all aspects like physical, mental, intellectual, spiritual and social. Details about all types of health are as follow:

Physical Health

1. Balanced dietary habits, a sweet breath and sound sleep.
2. Regular activity of bowel and smooth coordinated bodily movements.
3. Resting pulse rate, blood pressure, body weight and exercise tolerance are all within the normal range for the individual's size, age and sex.
4. All the organs of the body are of unexceptional size, and function normally.

Mental Health

1. Happiness, calmness, and cheerful demeanour.
2. Self satisfaction (no self condemnation or self-pity).
3. No conflicts within the self (no feeling of being 'at war' with oneself).
4. A balanced state of mind.

Intellectual Health

1. Accommodative intellect. Able to accept criticism, not easily upset.
2. Understanding of the emotional needs of others, considerate and courteous in all dealings, open to new ideas, possession of high emotional intelligence.
3. Self control. Not dominated by the emotions of fear, anger, attachment, jealousy, guilt or worry. Not driven by lust or greed. Able to face problems and solve them intelligently.

Spiritual Health

1. Possession of accurate knowledge and continuously experiencing awareness of the self as a soul. The feeling of such a self realised soul would be peace and purity.
2. Living without attachment to any object in the physical world including one's own body. A sense of brotherhood with other souls without coming under their influence. One's action will be elevated and characterised by integrity.
3. Constant intellectual communion with the Supreme being, by which positive energy is received and transformed into pure action. Self will be experienced by himself and others as humble, incorporeal and vice less. No worldly obstacles can affect him.

Social Health .

1. Forming friendships, which are satisfying and lasting.
2. Keeping family and social relations hearty and frictionless.
3. Acting for the benefit of the society in accordance with one's own capacity.

Soul Healing is the Whole Healing

Soul healing means getting rid of ignorance, wrong beliefs, peacelessness, anger, hatred, jealousy, pain, misery, lust, greed, ego and manifestation of truth, peace, love, contentment, purity, will power and bliss through our character and conduct. The seven primary virtues are the real forces behind the activation of our inner energy centres called *chakras*.

Until one has the knowledge of the soul and grasps completely that he has wrongly identified himself with the physical vehicle, which causes lack of the subtler forms of health, soul cannot rise out of the darkness in which he stumbles. *Rajyoga* practice is built upon this priceless knowledge of reality. **Thus Soul healing means the following:**

1. Practising truth in our life: which corrects all nervous systems, activates and purifies *AGYA CHAKRA*. A person suffering from neuro-disorder must practise truth in his life and visualise rays of deep blue colour around the face and brain cells during the *Rajyoga* Practice.

2. **Practising peace in our life**: which corrects our ENT problems, lungs problem, improves our power of speech and communication skills. A person with respiratory disorder should visualise peaceful rays of sky blue colour during *Rajyoga* mediatation. It activates and purifies *VISHUDHI CHAKRA*.

3. **Practising real love in our life**: which corrects our heart and lungs disorder, activates and purifies our heart centers *ANAHAD CHAKRA*. A person with CAD (Coronary Artries Diseases) must end hatred, jealousy and anger to manifest real love for all through his character and conduct. He should visualise green colour during *Rajyoga* exercise.

4. **Practising contentment in our life**: which corrects our digestive disorder, activates and purifies our navel center- *MANIPUR CHAKRA*. A person with digestive disorder must practise contentment and manifest joy and happiness through his behaviour. He should visualise yellow colour during *Rajyoga* meditation.

5. **Practising purity in thought, speech and action in our life**: which empower our immune system. A person with weak immune system and gynaecological/prostate problem must practise purity in his life and should visualise orange/saffron colour during *Rajyoga* meditation. It activates and purifies our *SWADISTHAN CHAKRA*.

6. **Practising will power in one's life**: which corrects bones and muscle disorder. A person with bones, muscle disorder and low confidence must enhance will power through *Rajyoga* meditation by visualising red colour during *Rajyoga*. It activates and purifies our root center–*MULADHAR CHAKRA*.

7. **Practising bliss in one's life**: which corrects endocrine system. A person with hormonal disorder must experience showers of bliss of violet colour during *Rajyoga* exercise. It opens and purifies the Crown *Chakra– SAHASTRAR CHAKRA*.

Thus, primary virtues are the key to open up our inner body energy centres, which in turn heal our physical bodies. **That is why, soul healing is called the whole healing.**

Following table explains the interconnections among soul's primary virtues, various energy centers of inner body, system of physical body, colours and various diseases.

TABLES OF PRIMARY VIRTUES AND CHAKRA RELATIONSHIP

Primary virtues of pure energy body (Inner body) & related consciousness and colours	Associated human system and related physical or meta-physical elements with virtues	Name of Chakra (Energy Centres in the physical body) associated with Primary Virtues	Position in the body and shape	Diseases in physical body due to lack of associated virtues and deformed mental body
1. **Power (Red Colour)** relates to our sense of survival & sense of grounding	Skeleton System, Physical **Element- Earth**	Muladhar Chakra, (Root chakra), or Pelvic or sacral plexus	Between Anus & Genitals, Shape-like **Four Petals** of Lotus	Diseases like Arthritis, osteoporosis, joints pain, muscular pain, sciatica etc.
2. **Purity (Orange Colour)** related with consciousness of pro-creation	**Reproductive & Immune system, Physical Elements- Water**	Swadhisthan Chakra (Hypo gastric or prostrate plexus or spleen chakra)	Between Navel centre & pelvic plexus (Root Chakra), Shape-like **Six petals of lotus**	Deficiency of immune system, (Aids), Gynecological diseases, problems related to prostate& kidney, and stiff or sore lower back etc.

3. Happiness or Contentment (Yellow colour) associated with control & leadership	Digestive system, Physical **Element- Fire**	Manipur Chakra (Navel Chakra) or Epigastria or solar plexus	Navel Centre Shape- like **Ten petals of lotus**	Acidity, gastric, peptic ulcers, constipation, gastrointestinal problem, diabetes etc.
4. Love (Green Colour) reflects consciousness of self-less love for all	Blood Circulatory system, Physical **Element- Air**	Anahat Chakra, (Heart Chakra) Or Cardiac Plexus	Heart, Shape- like **Twelve petals of lotus**	Coronary Arteries diseases, heart attack, angina pain, high B.P, lungs problem, asthma etc.
5. Peace (Sky Blue Colour) associatd with Communication skill and power of speech	Respiratory System, Physical **Element- Ether**	Vishudha Chakra (Throat Chakra) or Carotid or larynx	Throat, Shape- like **Sixteen petals of lotus**	ENT Problem, stiff neck, cough, colds, thyroid problem etc.
6. Truth &Knowledge (Indigo Colour) associated with power of intuition & balanced state of mind	Nervous system, **Metaphysical Element- Mind & Intellect**	Ajna Chakra (Medulla plexus)	Forehead (Between two-eyebrows) Shape- like **Two petals of lotus**	Nervous Disorder, decaying of brain cells, headache migraine, meningitis, ophthalmic diseases, blindness, strain etc.
7. Bliss (Violet Colour) associated with absolute Peace & wisdom	Endocrine System, **Metaphysical Element- Cosmic Power**	Sahasrar Chakra (crown Chakra) or cerebral glandplexus	Top of head (Crown), Shape- **Thousand petals of lotus**	Hormonal deficiency, depression, confusion, apathy, dullness, low IQ, EQ & SQ etc.

● ● ●

$\boxed{\textbf{14}}$

SCIENCE OF SUCCESS

Sleep Management

Sleep is the most important factor for a healthy living. The optimum hours of sleep one should have are between 5 to 7 hours. To manage our sleep, we must know the scientific fact.

Scientific fact about sleep: We sleep in cycles of 90 to 120 minutes each and our EEG indicates variety of waves during sleep ranging from alpha to delta. We spend first 50 % of each sleep cycle in light/very light sleep, next 30% in deep/ very deep sleep and rest 20% of the cycle in REM (Rapid Eye Movements) sleep (known as dream sleep).

We need to have a total of 45 to 50 minutes of delta waves to feel totally fresh after sleep. Our first two cycles carry about 20 minutes of delta waves in each cycle and the third cycle carries 5 to 10 minutes of delta waves only. After third cycle, delta waves are not produced at all.

Sleeping after third cycle is either due to habit or for psychological satisfaction. But it is a waste of time because it never gives you relaxations, instead it drains out gained energy during three cycles and people feel tired even after sleeping more.

Sleep after the third cycle is called half sleep or dream sleep, which produces more theta waves, which is a low amplitude wave with low frequency. So one need to have sleep only for three cycles. But two cycles sleep is also sufficient if needed. It freshens you up for next 12 hours. After 12 hours only you will feel to sleep one cycle, which again can freshen up for next 4 hours.

During deep sleep we sleep completely in delta waves, where as in theta wave sleep (dream sleep) our mind still works with imaginations but intellect does not function with its controlling power. Therefore, sleep means complete sleep with minimum 45 minutes of delta waves.

Brain waves chart: Brain waves are measured by an instrument named EEG (Electro Encephalo Gram). It measures electrical activities of the brain cells by placing electrodes on the scalp.

Sl no	Brain waves	Frequency	State of mind
1.	Beta	More than 13 Hz	Mind is alert & busy.
2.	Alpha	8 – 12 Hz	Mind awake but relaxed,
3.	Theta	4 – 8 Hz	Drowsiness, Dream state
4.	Delta	0.5 – 4 Hz	Deep sleep

How to manage sleep
1 By Relaxation technique or short nap:
Relaxation techniques produce alpha waves, which further reduces the rate of draining gained energy during delta wave sleep and keep us energetic as well as calm state of mind. Short nap of 20 to 30 minutes during daytime produces low theta waves and sometimes delta waves for 5 to 10 minutes, which refreshes us for next 4 to 6 hours.

2 By Rajyoga Meditation:
The theta and delta state of mind is achieved by *Rajyoga* meditation in which mind remains fully awake but cut off from external world or sense organ perceptions and connected to either inner self or supreme source of infinite cosmic energy.

Half an hour of meditation can give the relaxation equal to one cycle of sleep and refreshes us for the next six hours. 15 to 20 minutes of meditation can refresh for the next 3 to 4 hours.

Self Esteem

Self esteem means how do you feel about yourself. Raise your self-esteem to empower your mind.

Causes of low self-esteem:

1. Repetitive negative autosuggestion – I am weak, I cannot do it, I am not good etc.
2. Negative environment at home, in society and at work place such as talking about others, critical attitude, rebelling against the authority, flattery, confused and concerned about reputation, aggressive attitude, blaming others, selfishness, argumentative, enjoying vulgarity etc.
3. Valueless education and poor role model
4. Making unfair comparison and lack of discipline
5. Labeling by parents, teachers, superiors etc such as: you are dumb, you do not do things right, you cannot do anything in the life etc.

Do the followings to raise your self-esteem:

1. Talk about creative ideas
2. Have caring attitude, humility and be decent
3. Respect authority and others
4. Have courage of conviction and confidence
5. Be concerned about character
6. Accept responsibility
7. Take interest and remain optimistic
8. Understand others and have learning attitude

Positive Attitude

People, who are negative, never get anywhere and are invariably unsuccessful. Think positively and the world is your oyster. Think negatively and you are doomed to failure. Your attitude determines your altitude of success.

Reflect on the following true story: Wilma Rudolph was born in a poor family. At the age of four, she was suffering from pneumonia and scarlet fever. She came in the grip of polio also. She was using brace for her legs. Doctor had told that she would never walk in her life. But Wilma's mother encouraged her and said she could do whatever she felt like by the grace of God. Hearing this, Wilma told that she wanted to become a good runner in the world. Wilma took first step without brace at the age of nine. While doctor had told that she could never walk. At the age of 13 she participated in a running competition. She lagged behind many times. After that she kept on participating in other running competition until she became first.

At the age of 15, Wilma went to the State University, where she met a coach named Temple. Wilma told the coach her wish or ambition of becoming the fastest runner in the world. Then Temple said, nobody can stop you due to your will power and in addition I will help you.

Finally the day came when Wilma was participating in Olympics. In Olympic one has to compete with the best runners from all over the world. Wilma's competition was with Jutta Heine who had not been defeated yet. First run was of 100 meter in which Wilma won her first gold medal by defeating Jutta Heine. The second run was of 200 meter, in that Wilma again defeated Jutta and won second gold medal. The third race was of 400 relay races and again she had to compete with Jutta Heine. She ran so fast like a machine that she defeated Jutta continuously third time and won her third gold medal. And this incident was recorded in the history that after suffering from polio, a woman became the fastest runner of the world in 1960.

Fill up your mind positively to soar in the sky of success:
There was an old balloon seller who was trying to attract the attention of children by filling balloons with helium and letting them go up in the air. Looking at the coloured balloons, the children nearby pressurized their parents to buy the balloons for them. There was also a 10-year-old lean, black boy keenly watching these happenings.

After some time, he approached the old balloon seller and asked him, "Uncle I see the red balloon going up, the yellow balloon, the blue, the violet, and the white one but not the black balloon. Can this black balloon also go up like the other balloons?"

The old man was not as intelligent as you and I. He looked at the boy, thought for a second and understood as to why the boy had asked this question. He replied, "Son, the colour of the balloon does not matter. What matters are what is inside the balloon. If there is helium inside the black balloon, it would definitely go up."

He continued, **"Your caste, colour, religion, region and family background do not matter. If you have the right stuff inside you, i.e. self confidence, even you can go up in life and become a winner."**

These simple words of the old balloon seller changed the life of this young man, who went on to *become the greatest leader of the civil rights movement of the USA, Martin Luther King.*

Factors affecting our attitude:

1. Environment: Environment consists of homely atmosphere and peer pressures, workplace colleagues, superior and boss attitude, media comments by TV, newspaper, magazines, radios and cinema, cultural background, religions, traditions and beliefs, social environment and political environment.

2. Experiences: Our experiences affect our attitude. More and more experiences creates right attitude. We must be familiar with all types of situation in our lives.

When boat sails in the river in the different directions despite wind blows from uni direction only. This is because direction of the boat depends on how the 'sail' has been fitted which is decided by the sailor. We cannot change the direction but can choose how to fit the " sail" so that wind favours boat to reach to the edges. Similarly, in life we have to make certain choices to go against the odd. That is a tough choice but remember:

"When the going gets tough, the tough gets going."

" A hammer shatters glass but forges steel"

So we are neither glass nor iron, **any hammer of situation will forge us.**

3. Educations: Value based education helps to develop right attitude. Therefore we must pay attention for practicing values and virtues in our lives. We must nurture it through value-based education.

Steps for building a positive attitude:

1. Change focus (set your goal)

2. Make an habit of doing it now (stop procrastination)
3. Have an attitude of gratitude.
4. Educate yourself with values in life, which have five things: - *character, commitment, conviction, courtesy and courage.*

   "The first duty of a University is to teach wisdom and character not trade, not technician" –Winston Churchill.
5. Get away from negative influences of friends
6. Build a positive self esteem
7. Discriminate the necessary things from general things and do it
8. Start your day with prayer and meditation.

Reason for negative attitude–No Innovation:

Eight monkeys were locked in a room. In the middle of the room was a ladder leading to a bunch of bananas hanging from a hook on the ceiling. Each time a monkey tried to climb the ladder, all the monkeys are sprayed with ice water, which made them miserable. Soon enough, whenever a monkey attempted to climb the ladder, all of the other monkeys, not wanting to be sprayed, set upon him and beat him up. Soon, none of the eight monkeys wanted to climb the ladder. One of the original monkeys then removed, and a new monkey put in the room.

Seeing the bananas and the ladder, he wonders why none of the other monkeys are doing the obvious, but undaunted, he immediately begins to climb the ladder. All the other monkeys fall upon him and make him senseless. He has no idea why. However, he no longer attempts to climb the ladder.

A second original monkey is removed and replaced. The newcomer again attempts to climb the ladder, but all the other monkeys hammer the crap out of him. This includes the previous new monkey – who is grateful that he is not at the receiving end this time – and who does it because everybody else is doing so. However, he has no idea why he is attacking the new monkey.

One by one, all the original monkeys are replaced. Eight new monkeys are now in the room. None of them have ever been sprayed by ice water. None of them attempt to climb the ladder. But all of them will enthusiastically beat up any new monkey who tries, without having any idea why.

Don't be like those monkeys. Analyze your failure and set about correcting it instead of joining the pack and not saying something can't be done.

Do not satisfy your Ego:
Once a little fox found a bunch of grapes on a vine. Being hungry, he tried jumping to get to them, but they were out of his reach. Frustrate, he concluded they were sour anyway.

In the evening when his friends asked where he has been, he told them that he had found a vine of grapes but they were sour and hence he had not bothered. While his friends nodded in agreement, his grandpa, also listening to his story, did not support this. In the night he summoned the hungry young fox, *"Son, I see your ego has been fulfilled, but your desire is still unfulfilled."* This is not a bad state: go again tomorrow but this time; satisfy your desire, not your ego. *The trick is not to just try and try again, but if at first you don't succeed, try again, but try differently.*

The young cub followed the fox's advice and set out again. This time he tried other means, and after considerable effort he got a few.

"Grandpa," he reported later, "they are the sweetest grapes I have ever eaten. Tomorrow I shall go again and get the whole bunch." His grandfather just smiled. Motivation does not come from making a task easier, but from the sweat spent in making the result sweet.

"You never get what you expect,
Only what you inspect with respect"

Right Conditioning of Mind

Spiritual knowledge and Rajyoga – The Tool of Right Conditioning: In fact spiritual path gives us an opportunity to go into our conditioning aspect when we behave in a particular way, which we ourselves do not like. Sometimes we are forced to be obstinate, egoistic, jealous and so on. We try to examine our conditioning. Then we come to know that this is a wrong kind of conditioning we have got over a period of time. This has taken root in our subconscious mind. At this juncture normally we arrange for a self-directed conversation to ourselves. We tell ourselves that this is not the proper behaviour. We come to understand not only our own interest but also the interest of others and the world.

By practicing *Rajyoga* we substitute obstinacy with flexibility and adjustable nature, ego with humanity, jealousy with generosity, taunt with respect and regard. We tell ourselves: those are normal, generally acceptable and progressive feelings and we must have such a behaviour and feelings. Our conditioning starts changing towards this direction. We try to explore the perfect conditioning level as a human being. Humaneness should be the bedrock of any kind of behaviour. There is a humane level and divine level. Divine conditioning is the most appropriate and original level of conditioning. Our belief system turns topsy-turvy. 'I am not a body but a soul' makes all the difference. The consciousness change and undergoes a down to earth, positive, natural refinement and reconditioning.

Recondition your mind with the followings:

1. A little can make a difference

Let us take some water and heat it to 100 degrees centigrade of temperature. We call this water as boiling water. If we heat the water by one more degree, this boiling water turns to steam. Though the difference in the temperature is only one degree, the output of the boiling water and steam is vastly different. The great work that the steam can do is phenomenal. Remember, a little can go a long way.

2. Don't give up

Have courage and conviction when you are in deep trouble

One day, a farmer's donkey fell down into a well. The animal cried piteously for hours, as the farmer tried to figure out what to do. Finally, he decided the animal was old and the well needed to be covered up anyway. It just wasn't worth it to retrieve the donkey. He invited all his neighbors to come over and help him. They all grabbed a shovel and began to shovel dirt into the well.

At first, the donkey realized what was happening and cried horribly. Then, to everyone's amazement, he quietened down. A few shovel loads later, the farmer finally looked down the well and was astonished at what he saw. With every shovel of dirt that hit his back, the donkey was doing something amazing. He would shake it off and take a step up. As the farmer's neighbors continued to shovel dirt on top of the animal, he would shake it off and take another step up. Pretty soon, everyone was amazed, as the donkey stepped up over the edge of the well and trotted off.

Life is going to shovel dirt on you, all kinds of dirt. The trick to getting out of the well is to shake it off and take a step up. Each of our troubles is a stepping-stone. We can get out of the deepest wells just by not stopping, but stepping up, so never give up.

3. **Remember every blow matters**:

When you hit a rock with a hammer to break it, you might notice that nothing happens for the first many blows. But suddenly you hit it one more time. With the 100th blow, the rock breaks. Does it mean that all the 99 blows you hit previously were wasted? No, it isn't the 100th blow that knocks a strong rock down. It's the 99 that went before. Hence, you need to keep trying and never give up.

4. **Transformation is a process like metamorphosis, which makes a caterpillar (a worm) to become a butterfly**

It will be much relevant to quote Dr. Deepak Chopra regarding the biological transformation of the caterpillar into a butterfly. Talking about the collective transformation that is taking place in the world he said that the terrible situation in the world today provides an opportunity for the change. "One of the best examples of collective transformation is a process in biology called metamorphosis. It is something like a caterpillar becoming a butterfly. The two are quite different. The caterpillar is like a worm; the butterfly is a magical creature of beautiful colors that fly.

This is what happens: at some stage of its development the caterpillar becomes very greedy, it starts to consume more than it needs, when the consumption exceeds its metabolic needs, its body starts to die and starts to liquify. But within the body of the caterpillar there are few cells to which scientists refer as *"imaginary cells"*. These imaginary cells are literally dreaming a new reality. These cells vibrate in a different frequency of consciousness. When the caterpillar's body recognizes these imaginary cells, the immune cells of the caterpillar attack them. Because the imaginary cells vibrate at a different frequency, they remain immune to the onslaught. Soon the immune cells give up, and the imaginary cells start to gather in little clusters. Then something else happens, the clusters of imaginary cells start to connect with each other.

When the connectivity of these imaginary cells reaches a critical level, something magical happens. A gene, the genetic code that was lying dormant in the caterpillar wakes up, and in that genetic code is the information for wings, information for a new heart, information for the antennas, the information for legs, the information for a new metabolic rate the metabolism of flying creatures has to be different from the metabolism of a worm. *The imaginary cells start using the dying matter of the caterpillar as nutritive soup, it becomes the culture medium. The imaginary cells use to grow and to connect and soon the butterfly emerges with the flight to freedom."*

5. **Hero emerges from Zero**

Reflect on the following real story of a Great Personality of the world who became a "Hero from Zero":

When he was 7 years old, his family was forced out of home on a legal dispute.

At 9, his mother died.

At 22, he lost his job as a clerk

At 25, he was defeated in a legislature election.

At 27, he had a nervous breakdown.

At 28, he lost his beloved.

At 30, he lost the election for the post of a speaker.

At 35, he lost the Congress election.

At 46, he lost the Senatorial election – around the same time he lost his son.

At 47, he lost his Vice-Presidential elections.

These failures could not shake his self-confidence and at 52, he became the President of USA. That personality's name is "Abraham Lincoln."

6. Check the result:

Remember that there are **two sides of the results. That is inner and outer.** The inner results are the feelings and thoughts. The outer results are material things, conditions and relationship. To make real progress you have to check both.

It does not make sense to have all the money in the world and no personal enjoyment. Not does it make sense to be frustrated because of lack of money or success. Hence, don't wait for the perfect ladder or the perfect building. You will never find it. You will never make progress or create what you want in your life. Look for the ladder closest to you now and start to climb it. Check your results. Change ladders, or buildings, if needed to, the fact we will need to adjust things at some time or another. There is no ladder to happiness; happiness comes in climbing the ladder.

6. Think different to empower yourself

A boy used to come for football practice daily. But he was never included in the last eleven players of the team and always played as a reserved player. Whenever he came for practice, his father came with him and watched him playing.

Four days had passed when the match started but that boy came neither for practicing nor for quarterfinal and semi final. Suddenly on the day of final play, he went to coach, and said, "You have always kept me in reserve and you never allowed me to play in the team but today I request you to let me play the final match." The coach replied, "Son, I am sorry, I can't allow you to play because good players are already there in the team. Today in the final match I can't take a risk." The boy requested the coach again and again that he would keep his promise. The coach had never seen the boy requesting. He said, "Ok, go and play but remember I am going against my own better judgment. It is the question of our school's prestige. Don't break my promise."

The game started and whenever the boy found the ball, he scored a goal and became the hero of the match and his team won the match. After the end of the match, the coach went to boy and said, "How I would be so wrong in taking a decision in my life. I had never seen you playing so nicely before this. How did you play so nicely?" The boy replied, "Sir, my father was watching me." Then the coach looked at the place where his father used to sit but found nobody was there. After that the coach said, "Your father used to sit when you came for practice but today nobody is there. *The boy answered, "Sir, I have never told you a thing that my father was blind and he died just four days before. Today for the first time, he is watching me playing from heaven."*

7. **Know the easy and difficult things in the life**

Easy is to get a place is someone's address book,
Difficult is to get a place in someone's heart.
Easy is to judge the mistakes of others,
Difficult is to recognize our own mistakes.
Easy is to talk without thinking,
Difficult is to refrain the tongue.
Easy is to hurt someone who loves us,
Difficult is to heal the wound.
Easy is to ask for forgiveness,
Difficult is to forgive others.
Easy is to set rules,
Difficult is to follow them.
Easy is to dream every night,
Difficult is to fight for a dream.
Easy is to show victory,
Difficult is to assume defeat with dignity.
Easy is to admire a full moon,
Difficult is to see the other side.
Easy is to stumble on a stone,
Difficult is to get up.
Easy is to enjoy life every day,
Difficult is to give it real value.
Easy is to promise something to someone,
Difficult is to fulfill that promise.

Easy is to say we love,
Difficult is to show it every day.
Easy is to criticize others,
Difficult is to improve oneself.
Easy is to make mistakes,
Difficult is to learn from them.
Easy is to weep for a lost love,
Difficult is to take care of it so as not to lose it.
Easy is to think about improving,
Difficult is to stop thinking it and putting it into action.
Easy is to think ill of others,
Difficult is to give them the benefit of doubt.
Easy is to receive,
Difficult is to give.
Easy is to read this,
Difficult is to follow it up.
Easy is to keep a friendship with words,
Difficult is to give it's meaning.

Practise Spirituality in the Workplace

By spirituality, we mean expressing more humanity; it has no religious component or preference. This interpretation is important since each person has his or her own beliefs, which should be respected.

Spirituality is not something we should practice only when it suits us according to time and place. It should be cherished and cultivated wherever we go. And since we spend most of our time in the workplace, it is imperative that we take our spiritual values with us even where we work. *These values are creativity, communication, respect, vision, partnership, energy and flexibility.* All these seven are related, and all are important at our work places. Thus practicing spirituality means being as follow:

1. **Be creative:** Creativity includes the use of color, laughter and freedom to enhance productivity. *Creativity is fun. When people enjoy what they do, they work much harder.* Creativity includes conscious efforts to see things differently, to breakout

from habits and outdated beliefs to find new ways of thinking, doing and being.

Suppression of creativity leads to violence. People are naturally creative. When they are forced to crush their creativity, its energy force turns to destructive. Their inherent humanity must express itself.

2. Be communicative: Communication, communication, communication! This is the vehicle that allows people to work together. In our society, our learning process is based on learning to communicate with teachers and parents.

So when we come to the real world, this social conditioning leads us to resort to subterfuge – trying to figure out how to beat the system, gain extra favours, say the " popular" thing or to keep our views to ourselves rather than " rock the boat."

We should change this mindset and express what we feel about it without fear and let others know where we stand. It does not matter your views should match your superiors. Your peers will respect you as a man with principles.

3. Respect your colleagues: Respect of self and of others includes: respect for the environment; other people's personal privacy, their physical space and belongings; different viewpoints, philosophies, religion, gender, lifestyle, ethnic origin, physical ability, beliefs and personality.

When we learn to respect our peers, we accept their differences. We can learn to use those differences for our mutual benefit. For example, the person who can sit all day in front of a computer and be productive can help the person who works best by talking and moving around. Both functions are important. Rather than criticizing the other for being different, we can learn how different people see the world. *Lack of respect and acceptance lead to conflict and hostility.*

4. Have a vision: *Vision means seeing beyond the obvious – seeing the unseen.* It is a trait used to describe leaders and entrepreneurs. Where does vision come from? For some people, it is an inborn trait. They have always seen things that others cannot see. And, having seen the vision, they head straight for it. They follow their vision in spite of obstacles or non-believers.

5. Learn to be a partner: Partnership encompasses individual responsibility and trust that other people will perform according to their commitments for the good of the team and partners. *Partnership accepts that different people have different viewpoints and beliefs, those differences are used as positive aspects for broadening the team experience.*

Partnership encourages the female and male aspects of us to work together, without either one over ruling or dominating the other. *Lack of partnership lead to isolation and unhealthy competition.*

6. Be energetic: *Very positive energy forces are released when people feel creative, have the freedom to express their opinions, and feel respect from their management and their peers. The opposite energy force creates hostile workplace situations.* Your contribution to the collective positive energy is using your own creativity, communicating well, having respect for others, adapting to changing situations, working well with others and enjoying what you do.

Your contribution to the collective negative energy is withholding your talents, communicating without respect, fighting and arguing with others, resisting changes, creating tension with others and hating what you do.

7. Be flexible: Flexibility includes the ability to adapt to changing situations and allowing one's own beliefs and habits to change as needed. Learning to see trends and prepare for them is one way of learning flexibility. Another is to learn about our own strengths, our weaknesses and about self.

Determine the Purpose of Life – Goals

Everybody in this world is busy 24/7. From a rickshaw puller on the street to a big business magnate, if you ask them if they have any free time, the answer will be a big 'no'. If everybody works for such a long hours and keep themselves busy, then how come some people are successful and some aren't?

The same doubt once came to the students of a *gurukul* and they asked their master. The master did an interesting experiment.

He took a jar and filled the jar with some big rocks up to the brim, and he asked the students," is the jar full?" the students replied, "Yes, sir."

The master said, "No," and he put some pebbles in the jar. These pebbles tumbled in and occupied the little gaps left in the jar between the rocks. Now the master asked the same question to the students, "Is the jar full?" The students replied, "Yes, sir". The master said, "No." Then he filled the jar with some sand. The sand occupied the tiny spaces left between the rock and pebbles. Once again the master asked again the same question, "Is the jar full?" the students became very wise by now. They said, "No, sir. You can even pour some water into the jar." The master poured some water in to the jar. Now the master again asked, "Is the jar full?" The students said, "Yes, sir." The master said, "I fully agree with you. But tell me what do you understand by this experiment?" The students gave different answers.

Finally the master spoke, "Let us imagine that the jar is our life. The different things that we put into the jar are activities that we do in our day-to-day existence, which occupies our life. It is important, what we are filling our life with. Let us imagine that we do this experiment in the reverse order. If we pour water into the jar first, then the sand will not go into the jar. Even if we pour in the sand, the pebbles won't go in and finally, the rocks won't find a place in the jar at all.

Remember, the small pebbles, water and sand that you see are the activities that we do daily, like dropping or receiving somebody at the railway station, paying our bills, taking your bike for servicing, buying provisions from the shop, standing in a line to buy tickets, etc. The big rocks are the goals or the major objectives that we want to achieve in our life. Only if we spend our time effectively, only if we focus our energy on achieving these goals, can we become successful in our life. The rest of the activities will take care of themselves.

Everybody in this world is busy. But to become successful, we have to ask ourselves, "What are we busy with?" Like I said earlier, it is only when we ask powerful questions that we get powerful answers. The answers to these questions determine our purpose of life.

Ten Ways to Achieve Your Goals in Life

If you are ready to achieve your dreams and goals, no matter how big, take the following 10 steps – one at a time – to ensure a successful outcome every time.

1. **Choose your goal:** Choose goals those are consistent with your values and beliefs. Then regularly check to make sure that your thoughts and actions are in perfect alignment with them. You won't work toward goals that conflict with your values. You are unable to achieve your goals when your thoughts and actions are inconsistent with them. No matter how hard you work, your performance will be determined.

2. **Choose a strategic goal:** Choose goals that are strategic. High achievers know that strategic goals accomplish many outcomes. For example, training properly for and running in a marathon accomplishes a number of great outcomes. You will most certainly lose weight, reduce your cholesterol level, strengthen your heart, increase your energy and stamina and improve your outlook.

3. **Choose a purposeful goal:** Choose goals, which transcend purpose. The very highest achievers develop goals that serve a purpose much greater than just fulfilling their personal desires. These people hold grand visions and choose goals that reach far beyond their self-interests. They take on causes, develop careers and create businesses as vehicles for making a positive difference not only in the lives of their direct contacts, co-workers and customers. But in the lives of many others as well. When you choose and achieve goals with transcendent purpose, you leave a lasting legacy that makes this world a better place for all.

4. **Define your goal:** Accurately define your goals. What exactly do you want? Envision your goals, name them and put them and put specific numbers on them. No one can achieve an unclear goal. Be precise.

5. **Find a way to your goal:** You will reach goals that move or excite you and stimulate your imagination. You will reach goals that are meaningful and fulfilling. You will reach goals that are vital to your health and well being, to your family and to your future. When the 'whys' behind your goals stimulate, motivate and inspire you, you will find a way to achieve them.

6. **Write your goal:** Put your goals and the reasons behind them in writing. There is power and magic in writing down your goals and the reasons why you choose them. Record them on file cards and place the cards where you will see them throughout the day on the mirror, or on your desk beside your computer.

7. **Set a deadline to your goal:** Set a deadline. As with your objectives, have the courage to be exact in setting deadlines for their achievement. A pre-determined deadline provides the discipline required for achieving the goals.

8. **Check progress of your goal:** Set intermediate milestones. If you want to save Rs 60,000 in 12 months, set intermediate milestones of 5,000 per month. Setting smaller, specific intermediate goals delineate make achieving your ultimate goal far easier, and provides an efficient means of tracking your progress.

9. **Get a partner to support your goal:** Get a partner. High achievers understood the significant benefits of having at least one person who completely supports them and is part of their campaigns.

10. **Announce your goal:** Go public with your goals. Tell family, friends and colleagues about your goals and it's deadlines. Ask them to help you along the way and hold you accountable knowing that you have people for you as a powerful motivator. Set yourself up for a success by making a public commitment to reaching your goals on schedule. Celebrate intermediate victories. Reward yourself for the achievement of each victory along the way.

●●●

Now you can

Improve your Memory

Without problem
choose book of your favourite author
Biswaroop Roy Chowdhury

Rs. 150/-

One Minute Mind Memory

In the present spell of highly competitive time, where knowledge, qualifications and skills are so richly available is people, the next parameter which can decide the overall merit is memory. It is an art of quick retrival of what you have in the stock of your mind. Means what you have is alright, but what you can pull out instantly from your mind system, on the hour of need, is paid most. This book is designed to make your mind capable to earn that premium.

Rs. 195/-

Invisible Doctor

This book tells about the doctors, medical researchers, and the hundreds of other people who have used me to cure a huge variety of illnesses and combat even the most incurable diseases. The authors of the book Biswaroop Roy Chowdhury and B K Chandra Shekhar.

Memory Unlimited

This book is a collection of examples from various areas of science, commerce and arts showing how Advanced Mnemonics can be helpful in improving the learning speed.

Rs. 150/-

Memory, Mind & Body

Memory, Mind & Body is the masterpiece by a master mind. It is another magnum opus by the renowed memory master. Biswaroop Roy Chowdhury, whose amazing work Dynamic Memory Methods was a record-breaking bestseller of the millennium, running into several reprints in a short span.

Rs. 195/-

Dynamic Memory Methods

Dynamic Memory Methods is a bestseller on memory developing techniques. This book deals with the use of scientific memory techniques. This book deals with the use of scientific memory techniques for memorising faster and retaining it longer.

Rs. 150/-

Rs. 150/-

Impossible.. Possible...

This book is about change. Poeple by nature are status quoists. This book will tell you how you can change the way you think, act and behave. The chronic patients can recover, the habitual failures can turn around.

Vocabulary@100 Words/hr

Whether you are a businessman, or a student, if you want to remember everything this book is a must for you. It deals with how to improve concentration Memorising difficult biological diagrams.

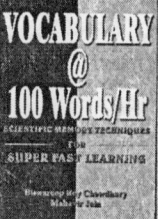

Rs. 95/-

Memorising Dictionary Made Easy

Memorising Dictionary Made Easy will be immensely useful to all. The book identifies every new word with a Key and Memory Link, which connect the new word with a more identifiable word and in the process get firmly lodged in the reader's mind.

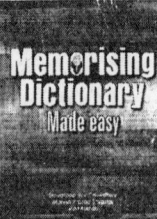

Rs. 150/-

Books can be requisitioned by V.P.P. Postage charges will be Rs. 20/- per book.
For orders of three books the postage will be free.

FUSION BOOKS — X-30, Okhla Industrial Area, Phase-II, New Delhi-110020,
Phone : 41611861, 40712100, Fax : 41611866
E-mail : sales@dpb.in Website : www.dpb.in